# YOU CAN MAKE YOUR DREAMS COME TRUE

# YOU CAN MAKE YOUR DREAMS COME TRUE

## Dale Hanson Bourke

Fleming H. Revell Company
Old Tappan, New Jersey

Scripture quotations in this book are taken from the King James Version of the Bible.

Library of Congress Cataloging in Publication Data

Bourke, Dale Hanson.
  You can make your dreams come true.

  1. Women—Religious life.  2. Women—Life skills guides.  3. Success.  I. Title.
BV4527.BB68  1985      248.8'43      84-13463
ISBN 0-8007-1216-1

To my parents,
who encouraged me to dream,
and to Tom,
who helps me make
my dreams come true.

# Contents

# *Preface*

It's a wonderful time to be a woman—at least that's what everyone says. Advertisers tell us we've come a long way, newspapers report new job options, speakers tell us we can be whatever we want to be. We can have a career or stay at home. We can marry and have children or we can remain single. We can be a corporate executive, a marathon runner, a soap-opera addict, or a full-time mom. We have freedom, liberation, options. And we have found that life can be very confusing.

We all remember the story of Midas in Greek mythology. Wanting to be rich, he asked the gods for the ability to turn whatever he touched into gold. But when his wish was granted, he discovered that it was a curse. He turned food into solid metal, a loved one became a statue, and his life was ruined by the unlimited freedom he thought he would enjoy.

As women we find that the doors that we once begged to walk through are now open to us. A woman can, apparently, go after anything she wants in life with minimal fear of discrimination.

In the pages of this book you'll meet many women—women who are struggling to find direction in life and women who have already taken responsibility for their lives. But the purpose of this book is not to introduce you to *them,* but rather to introduce you to *yourself.* Perhaps not the "you" you know today, but instead the "you" of your dreams.

This is not a book to make you feel guilty. It is a book of hope and expectation. It is a guide to helping you discover all you were created to be. And it is a book to help you realize how wonderful it is to be yourself in your given circumstances at this point in time.

This book is not a blueprint or a series of answers. Rather, it is a guide, a series of questions that only you can answer. The answers will be different for every woman. But the principles apply whether you're single or married, young or "mature," career or home oriented.

I wish I could tell you that this book is written by an expert. Unfortunately, it isn't. It is written by a woman who, like you, struggles with life's many options. A woman who feels the pull between family and career, freedom and responsibility, self-direction and total submission.

Together we will use this book to learn more about ourselves and to discover all we can be. My hope is that reading this book now and in the future will provide the incentive you need to keep searching for your direction in life. And my prayer is that this book will help you make all of your dreams come true.

# YOU CAN
# MAKE
# YOUR
# DREAMS
# COME TRUE

# 1. Where Are You Going?

When I was a little girl, my very favorite song was the Doris Day hit "Que Sera, Sera"—whatever will be, will be. I played that record on my portable record player over and over until one day I dropped it and "Que Sera" smashed into a thousand pieces. I can still remember how I felt as I begged my mother to glue the pieces together, even though the incident occurred more than twenty-five years ago.

Today, as I think back on the words to that song, I realize the message that came to me even as a small child.

> When I was just a little girl
> I asked my mother, "What will I be?

Will I be pretty, will I be rich?"
She told me tenderly,
"Que sera, sera
Whatever will be, will be
The future's not ours to see
Que sera, sera."

I thought about the future often when I was a little girl, usually imagining myself in the role of my favorite TV character or storybook heroine. But I never really *planned* for the future even as I matured. "Whatever will be, will be" summed up my attitude well. After all, didn't little girls just grow up, get married, have children, and live happily ever after? There didn't seem to be any other options.

Sometime during high school I began to realize that I'd have to make a decision or two if I were to move on to the next square in the game of life. I'm sure I tended toward the path of least resistance. Since most of my friends were college bound, I joined the pack.

But in college I was confronted with more decisions. Major? Class schedule? Roommate? Life-style? I remember feeling as though someone were playing a terrible joke on me. How could I decide among all these important options? What if I made a mistake? Why hadn't anyone taught me what to do? I quickly learned the sink or swim method of maturing.

Although the future might not be ours to see, it appeared that by treading water through life, the current would just drag me along. "Que sera, sera" meant my life would be determined by everyone except me. Doris Day or not, it didn't seem to be the way I wanted to live.

Then the "inevitable" happened. I met a boy and fell in love. My faith in the happily-ever-after theory restored, I began to envision my life as a wife and mother. I had just begun to notice china patterns, when our romance fizzled. After two years of "true love" I was once again faced with an uncertain future. And there were decisions and choices and frightening options. Where did I go after graduation? What did an English degree from a liberal arts college prepare me for? I scrambled, perhaps for the first time in my life, to pull together the pieces of who I was and where I wanted my life to be going. I read books, I asked for advice, I prayed—and I cried.

I thought about the way I'd lived my life thus far, with a "que sera, sera" attitude and a belief that my dreams would come true if I wanted them badly enough. I hadn't spent a lot of time preparing or planning or even defining what I wanted in life. As a result I found myself unprepared to cope with my current situation or my uncertain future.

In some ways I was fortunate. My first "life crisis" came early, when I was young enough to be flexible about my future. For some women, reality strikes later, when they have already established patterns for their lives and have responsibilities and commitments.

I was speaking at a writer's conference a few years ago when a woman approached me after my talk.

"Can I ask you a personal question?" the woman asked hesitantly, glancing around to make sure she was not being overheard. She was about fifty, with a look of desperation on her face.

I tried to give her an encouraging smile as I said, "Sure." I'd just finished a workshop on writing techniques and had answered questions on everything from the type of pencils I used to how to submit manuscripts to a magazine. I expected that she wanted to know something about my own writing methods.

"I hardly know where to begin.... You see, I came to this conference because I thought maybe I could be a writer, but I don't really know if that's what I want...." She took a deep breath and then started again. "The trouble is I don't seem to have any idea where my life is going. It all seems so aimless...." Her voice trailed off as she wiped a tear away. "You just seem like you know where *your* life's going. I thought maybe you could help me."

I was surprised by the woman's response to my speech, since it had been such an impersonal talk. And yet I saw in her eyes the same desperation I had felt when, as a college senior, I faced total uncertainty about my future. I understood that she felt as if she were drowning and was reaching out for anyone who could help her avoid being pulled under.

As we talked, I discovered that Ann had been happily married for twenty-five years, had two grown children, and, suddenly, a great deal of time on her hands. She had been drifting through life quite happily until now, letting circumstances determine her activities. But now she had to take a more active role in determining her future, and she simply lacked the skills necessary to make life choices.

Although I could give her few answers in the time we had together, I began to ask Ann a number of questions that I had found helpful in keeping me directed and on course.

"What do you want to do?" was my first and most obvious question to her.

"Why, I want to feel happy and fulfilled," she replied. We talked about the kinds of things she had done in the past that had made her feel happy, and slowly a common theme began to emerge.

Ann had loved her supportive role as a wife and mother. She enjoyed working behind the scenes, making clothes for her children, and encouraging her husband in his career. She couldn't imagine herself as someone in the spotlight and absolutely froze when faced with a leadership position. That was why she had come to the writer's conference. She thought that perhaps she could become a writer, since she could do it "behind the scenes." And yet she knew that she had no particular talent as a writer and wasn't even sure she liked to write.

Together we began to dream about all the other things she might do to help her feel happy and fulfilled and give her new direction in life. Some required more training or schooling. Others took little planning or initiative. By the time we had talked for half an hour she had scribbled notes all across a sheet of paper about ideas that she could pursue. When she stood and said good-bye, her face had completely changed. Instead of desperation she had a look of excitement. And instead of tears of despair, she had tears of joy. She gripped her sheet of paper with the scribbled notes as if it were her passport to the future, and, in a way, it was. It was the beginning of a journey that would take her as far as she wanted to go with her life.

As she thanked me I reminded her that I had done nothing more than ask her a few simple questions. The answers had come from her. The dreams and plans had been inside of her all the time. All she needed was someone to prod her and push her a bit to believe in her own God-given potential.

Later that same week I talked to a woman on the telephone who reminded me of Ann. Her name was Connie and she was only thirty years old. Yet she had that same sense of despair and longing. Although we were talking about a business matter, the details of her personal life began to find their way into the conversation, and I soon learned the source of Connie's unhappiness. It seems that Connie had graduated from high school with the same image I had of "happily ever after." She wanted nothing more in life than to marry her high-school sweetheart, have children, and become a home-maker. She was sure that it would be the most fulfilling role she could imagine.

At first everything went according to plan. She married Bob, whom she had dated for two years, settled into domestic life in an apartment, and later, in a house that they bought as Bob's career progressed. But try as they might, Connie did not get pregnant. Finally, after ten years and countless doctors' bills, Connie was faced with the fact that she would never have her own children. It was a devastating realization for her, since she had always been convinced that marriage and motherhood were what God had in store for her life. She had never pursued a career and had few interests outside the home.

Bob was not interested in adopting children, and he was beginning to pressure Connie to "do something with her life" so she would stop moping around the house and depending on him for emotional support. Meanwhile, she was sinking further and further into depression.

Connie's situation was, of course, more complicated than Ann's. Connie felt that she already knew what she wanted and that for some reason it was being withheld from her. As I talked to Connie, I tried to help her realize that life doesn't always happen the way we imagine it will; but that doesn't mean it has to be any less fulfilling. I reminded her of all the people whose lives had been changed by tragic accidents and who had learned to follow new paths within the confines of their handicaps. In short, I told Connie that she had to stop feeling sorry for herself and get on with life or she was going to be a bitter, lonely woman.

Connie admitted that I was right, but felt unable to cope with the many options facing her. Together we began to list some of the things she could do to take her mind off her problem and develop a plan of action for her life. Most of all, we agreed she needed to *do* something instead of thinking about herself. We discussed ways she could stretch herself mentally, spiritually, physically. I suggested some books she could read about setting and pursuing goals. Finally, we agreed that she would set a plan for herself and would accomplish something each week that would help her broaden her horizons beyond her home. "I'm going to call Bob at work right now," she said as she ended our conversation. "I know he'll be glad to hear that I'm willing to take the first step."

I wish I could tell you that Ann and Connie lived happily ever after. The truth is that I don't know what happened to either one of them. But I am quite sure that each took that first step in finding new direction in life. I suspect that by taking that first step they found so much gratification that the next steps were a pleasure rather than a chore. After all, life planning should be fun. It should be a challenge, but an exciting one that opens up new options and vistas. It should be a way to nudge and push you into taking responsibility for your own life instead of blaming unhappiness and confusion on "circumstances."

One of the wonderful benefits of my job as an editor is that I am often able to interview people whom I admire and ask them all the questions I want about their lives. Not only does it satisfy my curiosity, but it also teaches me how I can be like them. Of course some of the people I interview are wealthy or beautiful or talented because they were born that way. But I find that most "celebrities" I interview became successful through a combination of hard work, planning, and determination. When I interview women for *To-*

*day's Christian Woman* magazine, I often ask them what advice they have for "ordinary" women. Surprisingly, their answers are almost always along the lines of this: *Any* woman can be all she is intended to be. Live up to your God-given potential and you will be surprised at the amazing opportunities that open to you. You *can* make your dreams come true if you plan your course and set your sights on your goal.

One woman who is a good example of this is Mary Crowley, president of Home Interiors, Inc., a $400 million-a-year business. Mary faced her own "life crisis" when she was in her early twenties, and had two small children to support. She set out to get her first job without any background or skills and at the very worst time imaginable—during the Depression.

With characteristic optimism, Mary looked around her small Texas town and decided that she wanted to work in the nicest store in the area. Of course her initial application was rejected since the store was laying people off, not hiring. But Mary refused to give up. She insisted on talking to the owner.

Although the owner was impressed with her enthusiasm, he reminded her that because of the Depression he was barely able to keep the store open. But Mary had an idea. She offered to work for no salary for one Saturday. If she was able to generate enough extra sales to pay her salary, then the owner would hire her.

She spent the next days praying that God would help her find a way to sell enough items to cover her pay. And with His help she made a record number of sales on her first day of work.

Mary went on from there to set sales records in other companies. Then she moved into management and eventually started her own company. Today she primarily employs women in her sales force, and her words of advice come from her own experience: "You can be somebody," she says, "because God doesn't take time to make a nobody."

Another unforgettable interview for me was with Joni Eareckson Tada, an attractive young woman who became a paraplegic as the result of a diving accident as a teenager. Joni loved sports and had prepared herself for an active life, complete with a home and family. But then her tragic accident confined her to a wheelchair and left her unable to move from the neck down.

Of course, it was a time of crisis for Joni. Yet when I met this young woman more than ten years later, it was obvious that her reaction to the crisis had been constructive. She had taken positive steps in a new direction for her life. She began to share her experience with others and developed a ministry to those with handicaps. She studied the Bible and developed herself spiritually. She began to paint using her mouth, and to sing with the help of support for her weak diaphragm. She literally developed herself in every way she could.

Joni told me, "I choose to look at all that *can* be done, not at all the inconvenience. And that's my commitment: to turn a disability into an ability and a liability into a real asset."

Joni doesn't feel sorry for herself or even see herself as being very different from others. She says, "When you're disabled you're really no different than anybody else. We all tend to get self-centered to some degree or another."

My overwhelming impression of Joni was that she was an incredibly active, energetic woman. And yet, obviously, her energy was more mental than physical. She is a woman who is excited about where her life is going. If anyone has an excuse for passive living, it is Joni. But she has refused to live her life that way. Instead, she is becoming all she can be.

Joni is constantly making plans for the future and pursuing goals. She recently married and now even dreams of having a family.

Whenever I begin to feel sorry for myself or become lazy, I remind myself of Joni and her courage, discipline, and determination. I have no excuse for living my life passively. The only things that limit me are my own fears and my lack of discipline. If I can conquer my own constraints, I really can make my dreams come true. And so can you!

\*     \*     \*     \*

Take a minute to sit back and look at your life objectively. Ask yourself the following questions:

1. Do I know where my life is going? What are my goals?
2. Do I feel as though I am actively moving foward or am I just drifting?
3. Do I feel happy and fulfilled?

4. Am I blaming people or circumstances for keeping me from being all I can be?
5. Am I pushing myself mentally, spiritually, and physically?

Are you willing to take the first step toward becoming everything you can be? If so, you're ready for the next chapter.

# 2. Why Plan?

"**I** think it's wrong to plan for the future," a young woman told me after I finished a talk on life planning and time management. "If you start planning out your life, you become so regulated and rigid that you can't respond to others. Besides, so many things happen that you don't anticipate in life that it only frustrates you."

"It's true that you can overplan your life to the point of being rigid," I admitted. "And since life is full of unexpected detours, it's really impossible to predict whether your plan will ever come to pass.

"But I believe that we really have a responsibility to plan what we can, so that we *can* be responsive to the people and circumstances that come our way."

Life is a delicate balance between planned activities and unexpected circumstances. It is our job to plan for the future, make the most of what we have, and say yes to opportunity. God will bring along the unexpected.

Together the expected and unexpected will mesh into the fabric of our life. Without planning, the unexpected will control us and the fabric will be loose, messy, and the pattern will be hard to find. With too much planning the fabric will be too taut, controlled, and unimaginative. The proper balance brings beauty, harmony, and creativity. It gives us a framework in which to live yet gives us freedom to react positively to circumstances.

Proper use of planning, as I assured the young woman, doesn't make us robots. Neither does it make us selfish individualists intent upon our own pursuits. Instead it gives us a way to sift through the many options that come our way every day and allows us to choose with confidence.

Have you ever gone to bed at night feeling tired, but frustrated about all the things you *didn't* accomplish? All of us have days like that. I call them "mystery days" because somehow they mysteriously disappear without a trace. My mystery days usually start with my getting up later than my typical hour, finding nothing appropriate to wear, and generally feeling as though the day is going on without me. Mentally I'm just unprepared. I'm surprised when lunchtime arrives, shocked to realize that I haven't prepared dinner, and amazed when it's time to go to bed. I usually lie awake after a day like that and worry away an hour or two, thinking about how much more I'll have to do the next day to make up for my unproductive time.

I don't think there's anything that makes me more depressed than a mystery day. It makes me feel as if someone has robbed me of precious time, it makes me dislike myself for not being able to "get it together," and it makes me grumpy at those around me, who may or may not have contributed to my lost day.

Perhaps I'm a "type A," or very time-conscious person, but I have found many people share my frustration when they don't accomplish all they hoped to. No one feels good when the laundry is piled high, letters go unanswered, and the work in their "in" box begins to avalanche onto their desk. When days and weeks go by, undone work begins to eat away at self-confidence.

When I talk about life planning, I don't mean that it is a magic formula for righting all the problems in life. I really see it as a term that means coming to grips with what a person wants to be. It means daring to dream and then learning how to make those dreams come true. It means setting goals, managing time effectively, and moving from opportunity to accomplishment.

I truly believe planning can improve the quality of one's life, and that's why I think it's such an important concept. You may not be rich or powerful or beautiful, but you can be happy if you learn to make the most of yourself and come to terms with whom God created when He made you. Let's take a look at some of the specific ways life planning can help you.

## 1. *Planning gives you a sense of direction.*

I've heard of people who take their vacations by getting in the car, setting out down the highway without a map, and stopping when they feel like it. It always sounded like an intriguing idea to me, but I also think it's quite a gamble. After all, most of us have only two weeks out of the year to relax and get away from it all. It might be an interesting adventure, but I'm not sure how refreshed I'd be after a vacation like that. I plan my vacation time down to the last detail because I want to make the most of every minute of it. I feel the same way about life. I only have a certain amount of time and I want to live it fully. I'm afraid that coasting along will leave me frustrated and unproductive.

Planning provides a general scheme for days, years, even for an entire life. It gives me a goal to aim for; it highlights my path on a road map, and gives me an idea of my destination. It doesn't mean that I'll always end up exactly where I planned, but it does give me a feeling that I'm moving along in a way that is right for me.

As I look back, I see that the threads of my life have come together into a pattern I never would have anticipated. Because I was always interested in writing, it seemed natural for me to take a class in journalism when I was in high school. That class led me to work on the school newspaper, which I eventually edited. I learned then that I had a talent for newspaper writing, and I loved the deadline-oriented work. In college I naturally gravitated toward the school newspaper office and worked my way into the editor's role again.

Unfortunately, by the time I graduated from college, Watergate had made heroes of Bob Woodward and Carl Bernstein—and journalism was the most popular major in colleges and universities. I found myself in a huge pack of recent graduates trying to break into newspaper work. After a dozen interviewers urged me to brush up on my typing and try for a secretarial position, I finally got the message.

Fortunately, my writing background and my experience in a Christian college qualified me to work for an association of Christian colleges in Washington, D.C. I left the Midwest, where I had spent my life, and headed East to become publications assistant at the association.

After a year of working for the association, we began an advertising program to help attract students to our member schools. I became fascinated with the world of marketing and advertising and eventually left the college association to become a copywriter in a marketing firm. At that point it seemed that I had moved into an entirely new area and was leaving journalism behind.

Three years later, while working for a marketing consulting firm, a wonderful opportunity came my way. It combined my editing and marketing skills in an unusual manner and gave me the opportunity to edit *Today's Christian Woman* magazine. At the time I remembered thinking that only God could have put all the pieces together and ended up with such a perfect combination. As I work on the magazine, I draw upon experiences from all my previous jobs. I never fail to be amazed at how God knew what He was doing when He directed me first one way and then another. It seemed to me that I was going down a new path, but God could see the big picture. As I pursue the course set for me at this point, I always wonder what God has planned for me years from now. I know that it is my responsibility to head in the direction laid before me. God will take care of the rest.

### 2.  *Planning develops self-confidence.*

There's nothing that erodes my self-confidence more than feeling that I've failed. I don't even have to fail at something major. It might be a loaf of bread that didn't rise or a report that didn't get praised or an article that didn't get published. And I really begin to feel like a failure when I have too much to do in too little time, and I know that I'm not going to get it all done well.

On the other hand, I feel very good about myself when I've accomplished something—when I cross a job off my list or mail off a completed manuscript. I love the feeling of closure.

I have many hectic days, but some of them end with a tired, but satisfied, sigh, while others end in frazzled confusion. When I look at my day's "to do" list and know that I accomplished all my important jobs, I feel wonderful, even if I am exhausted. But when I end my day still trying to remember what I needed to accomplish, I have no sense of finality. I wonder whom I let down; what I left undone. That makes me begin to question what I'm doing and how well I'm doing it. And pretty soon I work myself into a state of depression, which eats away at my self-esteem.

Most of us think that confident people are just born that way. We all know people who seem to stride along unbothered and seemingly self-directed. Some of them are attractive or wealthy or powerful. But mainly they have an aura about them, making it seem as though everything is going their way.

If you take a closer look at self-confident people, you usually find that they have their share of problems. But most of them also have the ability to tell you what they want out of life. Have you ever thought about the fact that very few people have any idea what they really want? And even fewer people have taken the time to decide what they want and how they are going to get it. Such people have a certain confidence about them, however, that sets them apart from the crowd. Their goals aren't necessarily monetary or self-centered. They may be spiritual and altruistic. But when a person has a goal in sight and strives after it, there's a certain clarity and purposefulness about that man or woman that most people call confidence.

A few years ago the movie *Chariots of Fire* became overwhelmingly popular. It was the story of two men, Eric Liddell and Harold Abrahams, and the courses their lives were taking as they pursued their goals. Liddell was intent on becoming a missionary to China and was running because he believed that God had made him for a purpose and given him the talent to run. The actor who played Liddell did a very convincing job of showing the confidence this young man must have had. There was a quiet determination about him, a look in his eye that seemed to say, "I know where I'm going." No matter what circumstances occurred, he was a man whose single-mindedness could not be swayed.

Men and women like that are very attractive to others because they have a quality that people want to emulate. Their confidence makes them decisive and intent and usually earns respect.

One of the steps toward becoming a truly confident person is having a life plan. Once you know what you want to do with your life and begin to set your course, the many options coming your way become easier to analyze. You become decisive because you have already made your basic choices. And you develop self-confidence as you begin to move toward the goals you've established.

### 3.  *Planning gives you a feeling of accomplishment.*

When I look back at the years I spent in school, I realize how comforting it was to see a grade on my assignments. I knew exactly where I stood when I saw a "B+" or a "96" on a paper. Some teachers even went so far as to grade on a curve and elaborately plot the pattern on the blackboard after a test so everyone could see how their grade related to others in the class.

When I graduated from college, I soon discovered that there are very few ways to measure progress in the "real world." You can accumulate titles and money and clothes and awards, but rarely can you really tell how your accomplishments compare to those of others in an objective way. Of course people try to compare and measure their successes. Many people use a

Christmas letter to sum up the year's achievements: A new title; a redecorated house; a college degree; even a new pet signals a move up on the ladder of life. But there's always another rung above you and someone always makes more money or has nicer clothes or more brilliant children. Of course it would be wonderful if people could just forget about comparing themselves with others, but I think most of us really want to know how we measure up.

The only really important yardstick, however, is the one you establish for yourself. If you can learn to measure yourself against your own goals, you can learn to stretch yourself for your own sake, not for what the neighbors think or to beat out your friends. And ultimately, you'll be much happier when you achieve something that is really important to *you*.

My husband and I recently decided to establish specific financial goals for our young family. With the birth of our son we realized that our once-adequate financial planning needed to be improved to insure the security of our son.

We began by finding out just exactly where we were financially. That was the easy part. But then we had to decide where we wanted to be. Did we want to be as wealthy as the Joneses? Did we hope to be able to spend money as freely as the Smiths? We both agreed that we might envy the Smiths and the Joneses, but we had to establish a plan of our own that took into account our personal needs and desires. It wasn't enough to say that we wanted to do better than someone else.

Together we came up with a list that included goals such as an adequate retirement fund, money for our son's education, and a special fund that would enable us to take a vacation each year. After we finished establishing those goals, we set an amount that would accomplish each objective. Then we developed a plan whereby we would allocate part of our salaries to each of these funds.

Now if you ask me I can tell you exactly where we are when it comes to achieving our financial goals. We're a quarter of the way to paying for our son's education, a tenth of the way to having an adequate retirement fund, and we're taking our annual vacation next month. I have no idea where the Smiths and Joneses are, but I know exactly where we are, and it gives me a great sense of accomplishment every time I put part of my paycheck in the bank. When I'm tempted to spend money on clothes or something extravagant, I remind myself that I only have so many more dollars to place in the education fund before I fulfill my commitment for the year. That's often the only incentive I need to pass by the sale rack and head for the bank.

If you don't know where you're going, you'll never know if you have arrived. But if you do have a plan— one that you've established after a great deal of thought—your sense of achievement is greater with every step you take. You don't need to compare yourself with the neighbors, because their standards may be very different from yours. Your feeling of accomplishment will come from the grade you give yourself.

### 4. *Planning confirms and strengthens your priorities.*

Most of us spend the majority of time doing things that never contribute to our true goals in life. That's a startling realization that sometimes hits people at mid-life. A businessman may wake up one day and realize that he's spent twelve hours a day at work when his family and friends are really more important to him. A woman may see that maintaining a spotless house has kept her from pursuing another interest. These standard "mid-life crises" are just a realization that life isn't going the way we hoped it would or that we have misjudged our priorities. There's a gap between the real goals and the time spent on other objectives.

It's easy to get sidetracked from the things that you truly value and the priorities you establish. Every day there are literally dozens of options and causes vying for your time and attention. Some seem urgent. Others seem attractive or exciting. How can you possibly choose?

By establishing a life plan you can help yourself make those many decisions and choices every day. Once you've established your priorities, the options either contribute to your goals or they don't. It's really that simple. And if you constantly choose to do things that don't contribute to your stated priorities, it's time to admit that your *real* goals may be different from what you think they are.

I'm the type of person who needs to plan because I

can very quickly lose sight of what's important to me. I love new opportunities more than current projects. Every new idea sounds promising. Every potential story gets me more excited than all the articles I've already written. But the problem is that many new projects aren't opportunities at all. They're really traps that will ensnare me and keep me from concentrating on my established path. I can spend an entire afternoon working on a new dessert recipe. That's fine, but when six o'clock rolls around and I still haven't thought about dinner, it becomes clear that something is wrong with the way I have spent my time.

Karen is a friend of mine who is a very organized, hardworking woman. Soon after completing school she took a job with a prestigious company, where she worked long hours and was quite successful. But when she became pregnant, she knew that her child would become a higher priority than work. After taking time off for her son's birth, Karen returned to the firm part-time. That meant that she was no longer on the "fast track" or in line for promotions. But that was fine as far as she was concerned. Her priorities had changed and the excitement of the next title or the bigger office no longer tempted her.

On her two days each week at home she devotes herself to her son: taking him to the park, playing with him, and generally making him her primary concern. She admits that those days are difficult for her because she is so used to a fast work pace. She often feels that she should be "accomplishing" more during those days. But instead of giving in to that feeling she reminds herself that those are days to be spent with her son and it's more important to play with him than it is to devote time to work.

Planning keeps Karen from giving in to work pressures just as it keeps me from spending so much time on a new dessert recipe that I never get around to making dinner. It reminds us over and over of the reasoning underlying our actions and makes our actions consistent with our priorities. Planning helps us become the people we *really want* to be.

### 5. *Planning helps you to be flexible.*

Probably the greatest criticism I've heard against planning is that it makes you into a rigid, structured person who can't respond spontaneously. I'm sure that can be a problem in some cases, but I believe proper planning makes you a *more flexible* person. How can that be? I believe that people who plan their lives in the first place get more accomplished each day. And they spend most of their time on the more important things. That means that when some new experience or precious moment occurs in their life, they don't have to worry about all the important things they're not doing. Their life is basically under control. They know their priorities. And they know that time taken to enjoy a moment now can be made up later through proper planning.

Many people actually schedule time for the unexpected or to make phone calls just to say hello. During those times they can be totally open to others' needs and responsive to any circumstances. They know that the unexpected is often as important as what is planned.

All of us want to be flexible—to a certain degree. If my year-old son needs a hug and attention and my schedule says that it's time to make the beds, my son will almost always get the attention he needs at the time. But if my neighbor calls and wants to chat about something, I may ask if I can return the call in half an hour. By then I'll have those beds made and the house under control and will be able to concentrate on what she has to say without wondering how long she's going to talk.

For me, planning helps to clear my mind and gives me the freedom to think about the things I need to concentrate on. Once I've established my goals, set my priorities, and planned my time, I don't have to go through the process each time a new circumstance comes along. I'm totally flexible when my son is involved because he's high on my priority list. I can be flexible when a friend wants to shop if the trade-off isn't too great. A shopping trip will probably mean that I'm not accomplishing something else, but it's a choice I make with an understanding of the trade-offs involved.

Planning keeps me from feeling frazzled and nervous about what I might be forgetting, and that makes me feel good about the time I spend on both scheduled and spontaneous activities. It gives me a sense of order and an understanding of priorities.

Of course planning isn't the answer to all of life's problems. But for me it's an important element in realizing my full potential and knowing I'm doing my part to be all God created me to be.

\*     \*     \*     \*

In considering the role of planning in your life, ask yourself:

1. Do I ever feel frustrated by my inability to get things done?
2. Do I have a general sense of direction or do I feel as though I'm wandering?
3. Do the people I know who seem confident know what they want? Do they seem sure of where they're going?
4. How do I measure accomplishments in my life? Do I often compare myself to others?
5. Do I spend most of my time on the important things?
6. Do I regularly have to make decisions about the best use of my time?
7. Do I feel frustrated by interruptions? Do I know what trade-offs I can make each day?

# 3. *What Would Make You Happy?*

I had worked with Holly for less than two months, but in that time it became clear that she was a very unhappy person. Some days she walked into the office looking as though she'd just lost her only friend. She was overweight and growing heavier every day and her clothes were often wrinkled and spotted. She rarely smiled. And whenever the boss was gone, she'd come in late, leave early, and take long lunch hours. Although her behavior frustrated the rest of the staff, none of us ever told the boss about her. I guess we thought she was miserable enough already, and we didn't want to make life any worse for her. But none of us went out of our way to befriend her, either, and Holly never seemed interested in anyone other than herself.

Then one day Holly walked into my office, dropped some papers on my desk without a word (her usual behavior), and started to walk out. For some reason, I asked, "How's it going?"

Holly turned around with the most miserable look on her face and snapped, "Terrible."

"Want to talk about it?" I ventured.

Holly looked at me for a long moment and then started to cry. "I'm just so unhappy," she sobbed.

After a while Holly calmed herself a bit and I decided to try a more positive approach. I asked her what would make her happy.

She looked at me with a confused expression and said, "I really don't know. I just know how miserable I am right now and how unhappy I feel."

We talked several times after that, and I tried to help Holly think about what would make her happy and help her to feel better about life. It wasn't easy. Holly had spent so much time concentrating on what made her miserable and what she lacked that she'd nearly blocked out the positives in life. She had a very difficult time learning to dream about the person she could be.

Many of us are a lot like Holly. We may not be as deeply troubled as she was, but we can easily list all the things that make us unhappy with ourselves and our lives. And yet when it comes to imagining what would really make us happy, we find that we're unable to give a concrete answer. We've buried ourselves under all the things we aren't.

That's what this chapter is all about. We're going to learn to dream, to think about everything we've always wanted. We're going to make a "Christmas list" for ourselves on which we write down all those big and little wishes. We're going to learn to shake ourselves up a bit and look into those secret hopes and dreams that we've been burying under the bushel of our daily chores.

Does dreaming sound selfish to you? Are you afraid that your wish list will make you seem self-absorbed and materialistic? Please give it a chance. This is an exercise designed to help you understand yourself and what you really value. Obviously, you're not going to be able to make *all* your dreams come true, but you are going to learn what some of your dreams really are and what options you can choose from.

Take out a clean sheet of paper and write at the top of the page, "What would make me happy?" Then spend ten minutes writing down everything you can think of that would make you feel good. Don't worry if some things seem trivial while others are important. Don't worry if you list things that seem impossible. You won't have to show this list to anyone, so be as open as you can with yourself and list as many things as possible.

My list ranges from "a new nose" to wishes for my marriage; from "the navy blue skirt I saw at Bloomingdale's" to hopes for my son; from two famous people

I'd like to meet to more time to read the Bible. All of these are things that would make me happy—some momentarily and others in a deeper, more lasting way. At this point that distinction doesn't matter. This is just the first draft of my wish list.

The rest of this chapter will help you expand on your wish list. It will help you go beyond some of your built-in barriers to become all you can be. As you read the rest of this chapter and think about it, keep your wish list in a file folder and add to it. Also use the file to drop in magazine and newspaper clippings and other brochures or pictures that spark your imagination. Every time you read about someone you admire or see an appealing vacation advertisement or get an enticing catalog from a store, drop it into your file. Once again, don't limit yourself to those things you think you *should* want. Collect everything that interests you in this dream file without any self-criticism.

### Learning to Think Big

One of the greatest difficulties women have is learning to think big. Most of us are so caught up in daily routines and chores that we have a hard time looking at the big picture and seeing the truly important things in life. We often suppress our dreams because we fear they will only make us unhappy with the situation we're in.

I don't think that's healthy or wise. I believe God gave you your hopes and dreams for a purpose, and by exploring them you can glimpse your potential and move closer to what God intended you to be. You may find that some of your hopes and dreams tell you that the way you're living is different from what you really want. That doesn't mean that you should leave the laundry piled high while you run off to take opera lessons. You will still have choices to make further down the line when you learn to make the necessary trade-offs in your life plan. But for now it's important to learn to look at all the things you dream about. Here are three steps to get you started in your thinking:

1. *Overcoming inhibitions.* Whenever I hear someone say anything about inhibitions, I imagine a stereotypical little old schoolteacher with a high neckline, hair pulled straight back, wearing "sensible shoes." But the fact is we're all inhibited in one way or another by the different experiences of our lives. Of course it isn't desirable to get rid of all our inhibitions and assume a "do your own thing" mentality. But we need to look beyond some of the restrictions placed on us by others and ourselves in order to learn to dream our own dreams.

Probably most inhibitions are rooted in childhood and early family experiences. You may have been told that girls don't play with trucks or that college is for boys. Although you may have grown up and discovered that those "truisms" weren't so true after all, psychologists tell us that those childhood "tapes" play the messages back to us and influence our thinking for a long time. You may have been told that you were funny looking or gawky or loud. Do those statements still influence you?

When I was a girl I grew quickly and by the time I was in sixth grade I was the height I am today—five feet five inches. I was taller than most of the boys in my class and I felt like a giant. I always thought of myself as a "big person." One day, just a few years ago, a friend was shopping with me and suggested I try on a brightly colored dress. I laughed and told her that I only wore dark colors because I was so big. She looked at me strangely and asked what I meant. Pointing out that I was of average height and weight, she asked what made me think of myself that way. I realized then that I was still carrying around an image of myself from fifteen years before. I was letting that inhibition keep me from seeing myself clearly and exploring my options.

There are all kinds of ways that we are restricted by others and held back from thinking big. Sometimes our circle of friends holds to a certain viewpoint. Women who work might have the attitude that women who are homemakers are not as hardworking or productive. Some homemakers, in turn, believe that women who work are selfish and don't care about their families. If most of your friends hold one of these views, it's very hard to consider whether you should work or not without fearing their judgment.

Sometimes your church influences your thinking in ways that go beyond theology. Some churches place a great deal of emphasis on community service and helping the disadvantaged. Others emphasize personal spiritual growth. If your church has no community-outreach program, you'll really have to make an effort to serve in that way if it's what is important to you.

It's essential to look closely at all the ways you have been and continue to be influenced by others. It's certainly all right to agree with the opinions of others, but it's very important to think and dream for yourself. Only you know what you really want and what God created you to be. You can't let others limit you to their image of you.

2. *Readjusting your attitude.* Probably the greatest problem women in general struggle with is lack of confidence and a negative self-image. Because of that we begin to tell ourselves that we don't deserve to succeed or we aren't good enough to live up to our hopes and dreams. But I've found that a negative attitude will limit you more than lack of money or talent or any other resource. A positive attitude can help you succeed beyond your wildest hopes and dreams. With a positive attitude you can think bigger than you've ever imagined.

How can you develop a positive attitude? Begin by following the biblical advice: "Whatsoever is good, think on these things" (*see* Philippians 4:8). Negative thoughts and people feed on one another. Have you ever been with a group of people who were critical or very negative? If you try to say something constructive or positive, you're a traitor. The only way to get along with people like that is to be negative and critical yourself. The more you say, "It can't be done," the more you believe it and limit yourself to being less than you can be.

Surround yourself with people who are positive, creative, and excited about life. Look for the good in others and refuse to join in criticism. Read positive-thinking books and listen to tapes by people like Norman Vincent Peale, Robert Schuller and Zig Ziglar. After a while you'll find your dream list expanding as you increase your creative energy and dare to dream of things you never before thought possible.

3. *Giving yourself a chance.* One day I watched a ballerina dance across the stage, and something inside me wanted to jump and twirl as she was doing. I immediately suppressed the thought, but later retrieved it from my subconscious. Could I someday become a ballerina? Probably not, given the time and training necessary, but the fact is I'd never even given myself a chance. I'd never taken a dance lesson in my life and I'd never pushed myself physically. It was wrong to limit my dream without exploring it.

One day someone asked me if I'd ever wanted to write a book. "Nope," I answered honestly. I'd never really thought about it but couldn't imagine undertaking such a challenge. A few months later someone else asked the same question. I realized then that other people had more faith in me than I did. Could I write a book? I didn't know. But I decided to give myself a chance. What you are reading is the result of a difficult process but also the realization of a new dream. I could have kept telling people that I couldn't write a book, but instead I gave myself a chance. Now I know that writing a book is something I can do; it's potential that I had within me for a long time and just didn't realize.

With adult-education classes and teaching tapes and correspondence classes readily available, it's possible to be introduced to and explore so many areas in which you may have an aptitude. With most things you don't just demonstrate a talent without first knowing the basics.

God may have given you musical abilities that will remain untapped if you never take beginning piano lessons. You might be a gourmet cook some day, but first you have to learn basic cooking techniques. The point is that you shouldn't be limited in your dreams by not giving yourself a chance. You'll never know what you can do if you don't try.

### Looking at Your Options

With all the world available to you how can you find your real interests? Once you've overcome your inhibitions and negative attitudes and are willing to give yourself a chance, how do you discover what the world has to offer? Begin by following three steps:

1. *Expanding your horizons.* Every one of us has certain cultural and social boundaries in our life. In order to really dream big dreams we need to take a look beyond our own little world and explore brand-new options.

You don't need to sign up for a safari to expand your world. You can begin by reading your daily paper with an eye toward interesting people and new options. Recently I realized that the news was full of stories about the Middle East and I didn't even have a good mental picture of the region and how the countries related to one another. I studied a map, which helped me understand border disputes and increased my desire to learn more about the region. I read a popular novel by John le Carré, *The Little Drummer Girl,* which further intrigued me. Recently I added "visit the Middle East" to my dream list. Although I'd never thought of it a few months ago, I am now intrigued by the thought of seeing that part of the world.

Another way to expand your world is through adult-education courses or classes offered through a nearby college. Why not take a class in French cooking or sign up for a seminar on Asian art? Who knows what will spark your imagination and start you dreaming?

One of the very best ways to expand your horizons is through the people you meet every day. Dale Carnegie said that there is something to be learned from everyone you come in contact with each day. He suggested that developing an interest in others is a key principle in learning to win friends and influence people. It's also a good way to find out firsthand about others' dreams and to see if they interest you.

On a beautiful summer day a postman came to our office in his Bermuda shorts whistling a tune. "Do you enjoy your work?" I asked. "Love it!" he said without hesitation. "It keeps me in shape, and I love working outdoors even in bad weather."

Soon after that I added "outdoor work" to my dream list. Although I had no desire to be a mail carrier, that postman had stirred in me a love of the outdoors that had been forgotten after years of office work.

2. *Asking questions.* One of the most frustrating stages for any parent is when a child begins to ask "why?" Every statement is questioned; every fact is challenged. Unfortunately, most of us move out of this childhood stage, become responsible adults, and rarely ask "why?" again.

Learning to ask "why?" and "why not?" can help you broaden your thinking and expand your dream list. Begin to question your daily routine, the way you wear your hair, the kinds of books you read. Have you fallen into a rut without even realizing it?

Then learn to ask "what if . . . ?" What if you didn't have to worry about vacuuming every Thursday? What if you were a size 8 instead of a size 12? What if your house looked as if it were taken from the pages of *Architectural Digest?* What if you took a course on computers? Would any of these things make you happy? If so, add them to your dream list.

If you have a close friend who can help you play the question game, have her ask you questions about your dreams and aspirations. She'll probably come up with areas you've never thought about and you may do the same for her. Remember, the point is to think about every conceivable dream; to list every secret hope.

3. *Stretching yourself.* Most of us have a mental image of ourselves that defines who we are today. But few of us carry a picture in our minds of who we'll be tomorrow. Close your eyes and imagine the ideal you a year from now. How do you look? What job do you have? What are you interested in?

In my mind I see a smiling woman who is tan and

slightly muscular. I'm wearing a tennis dress and serving remarkably well. When I miss a point, I'm calm and never lose my temper. My son is playing happily by himself and my new car is parked in the lot. Although I'm not there today, that's the woman I dream of being. I'd like to play a respectable game of tennis and I hope to trade my flab for muscles. I want to learn to control my temper. I'm imagining that my son will learn to amuse himself and give me more time to pursue other interests without constant attention. A new car? Maybe. It's not something I think about that much, but while I'm at it, I'll add it to my dream list.

With that image of myself in mind it's a lot easier to remember to do my sit-ups and pass that dessert by. If I can hold on to the image I *want* to be, I'll begin to push myself today to become the woman of my dreams.

One of the most significant things I ever heard was a simple question by Robert Schuller, "How would you live your life if you knew you could not fail?" What a thought! Imagine knowing that you could attempt anything and succeed. You could knit a sweater without dropping a stitch. You could cook a soufflé and not worry about its falling. You could enter a marathon and complete the race.

What would you attempt if you knew you could not fail? Probably nothing that you couldn't attempt now without a reasonable chance of success. But by removing the risk you might attempt things that were a bit more daring or slightly more challenging.

Add all those things to your dream list (which should

cover more than a page by now). Study the list and think of all the opportunities that lie ahead. Those dreams aren't so crazy, you know. If you really want to you'll be able to achieve many of them.

\* \* \* \*

As you learn to dream, ask yourself:

1. What will make me happy?
2. What messages from childhood keep me from thinking big?
3. How do other people's opinions and prejudices keep me from dreaming my own dreams?
4. Do I spend too much of my time with negative people?
5. Do I think negative thoughts more often than positive thoughts?
6. Am I giving myself a chance in new areas? What have I never tried that I might enjoy?
7. What am I doing today to expand my horizons?
8. Am I questioning the "givens" in my life?
9. Do I have a mental image of what I'd like to be?
10. How would I live my life if I knew I could not fail?

# 4. *Where Are You Now?*

After developing your dream list, you might want to pause in your reading. You've probably imagined all sorts of wonderful things that you want to fantasize about for a while. That's fine. The next chapter is designed to help you sort through your dream list and begin to develop a plan to make some of your dreams come true. If you're not ready for the next step, keep dreaming for a while. There's nothing wrong with collecting and enjoying your hopes and dreams.

Your dream list is something that will keep expanding as your interests change over the years. Your dreams will keep you excited about tomorrow. They'll help you keep growing and stretching. And they'll become promises you make to yourself for the future.

Just as your dreams give you hope for tomorrow,

what you've already done in your life can give you a better sense of yourself today. Analyzing who you are and what you've accomplished can give you the confidence you need to take that next step. Assessing your life so far will help you see patterns that are already there. And getting a firmer image of who you are can help you understand more about who you really want to be.

Early in my work experience I was assigned the job of managing two other employees. The thought of being responsible for managing others terrified me, and that fear, combined with my inexperience, made me act like a little general instead of a supportive boss. As the working situation went from bad to worse, I began to lose my self-confidence, hate my job, and even hate myself. I felt like a miserable failure, and I wondered why I had ever thought of pursuing a career. I had just about convinced myself that I would never hold a responsible job again, when my boss called me in for a talk.

He was a wise man in many ways, and, although he was as aware of the problem as I was, avoided confronting me head on. Instead he asked me questions about my childhood, how I related to other children, and what I'd enjoyed during school. Then he said, "You know, I can see from your background that you're really something of an individualist. You're creative and energetic and you like to take the ball and run with it. Those are very important talents. I think I've made a mistake by making you spend so much of your time in management and so little in areas where I know you have proven skills."

It was the kindest "reprimand" I'd ever received, but my boss went beyond that. He showed me what I probably had known all along—I had always been more of a project person than a people person and my management talents were virtually nonexistent. That didn't mean I'd never be a manager, but managing wasn't a natural talent of mine. If my career plans called for moving up the ladder in a corporation, I'd have to work on learning those skills. However, it might be that I should pursue a career in which being a good manager wasn't an important factor. Being deficient in management skills didn't make me a failure, I began to understand. I didn't have to lose confidence in my overall abilities because I lacked experience and natural talent in one area. I began to readjust my career dreams to include what I knew I enjoyed and tried to pursue work goals that helped me learn to be a manager.

We've all heard that people are as different as snowflakes and that God created each of us to be a unique human being. But then we spend so much of our lives trying to look, sound, and act like everyone else we know. That's bound to make us unhappy at times because, depending on our individual talents and interests, we may find ourselves "out of style." We may have curly hair when straight is the fad. We may be the quiet type when all the people we know at the office like to party. We may like to pursue interests at home when every other woman on the block seems to have an exciting career.

It's so important to understand that there's nothing *wrong* with being who we are. God made us that way for a purpose. He gave us our interests and talents and likes and dislikes and formed them in a combination that is unique for each of us. As we begin to look to the future we must learn who we are already and what dreams will help us move closer to what we can be.

### Getting to Know Yourself

With the growing use of video recorders, many people are learning to become better public speakers, tennis players, and golfers simply by watching tapes of themselves. Just by accurately viewing themselves, they can learn to correct the behavior that has kept them from moving on to the next level of expertise. I suspect that if each of us could watch a movie of our life so far we'd be struck by our behavior. We might notice how often we're in a hurry or how many times we laugh or even how we receive compliments but brush them aside. Taken together, the events of our life would give us a better picture of who we really are.

Unfortunately, the picture we have of ourselves is often colored by what our scale told us this morning or what our neighbor criticized us about yesterday, or how our dinner turned out last night. It's difficult to step back and put it all in the perspective of a lifetime.

This is a practical, hands-on section, so use a pencil to fill in the blanks, or use a separate piece of paper to answer the questions in the following exercises.

You'll work hard on the exercises in this section, but please stick with it because your answers here are essential to helping you make your dreams come true.

## Exercise #1

*How do I view my life?*

Once when I applied for a job, I was asked to answer some questions designed to help my potential employer understand me better. One of the questions asked me to draw three circles representing my past, my present, and my future. Take a minute to draw three circles that represent *your* life in terms of the past, present, and future. Don't turn the page until you have drawn your circles and taken a moment to think about what they represent.


PAST             PRESENT             FUTURE


Is your past circle largest? Are you spending time looking back at where you were?

Is the present circle the largest? Are you so caught up in today that you can't imagine the future?

Is your future circle the largest? Are your plans for tomorrow more exciting than your life today or what has happened to you so far?

There are no right or wrong answers to this exercise. But by completing this simple test you can learn something about your perspective on life. What I hope to do is show you what your past has taught you and what you can learn from today so that you can make your future circle bigger than your past and present combined.

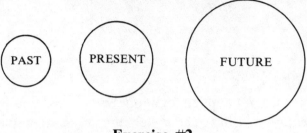

PAST     PRESENT     FUTURE

**Exercise #2**

*What do I enjoy?*

Have you ever watched Barbara Walters interview celebrities? She loves to ask them all about their daily life, what they like and dislike, and how they feel about themselves.

Let's pretend Barbara Walters is interviewing you for a TV special. The following is a list of questions that she might ask. Jot down your answers after the questions or write them on a separate sheet of paper. Don't write what you think you should say. Be honest. The point of this exercise is to get to know who you are, not what others want you to be.

1. What kinds of books do you like to read? (suspense, romance, biography, etc.)
2. What magazines do you like to read?
3. What are your favorite television shows?
4. What movies have you enjoyed most?
5. What leisure activities do you enjoy?
6. In what type of clothes are you most comfortable? (business suit, blue jeans, jogging outfit, etc.)
7. What type of music do you enjoy?
8. What is your favorite sport?
9. What type of work do you enjoy?
10. What relaxes you?
11. Whom do you admire?
12. What famous people would you most like to meet?

13. What is your favorite time of day?
14. Who are your favorite people?
15. What do you like most about yourself?

Take a minute to review your answers. What have you learned about yourself and your preferences?

I've reminded myself that I love to listen to jazz music and that a bubble bath relaxes me. My favorite time of day is early morning and I enjoy active work.

The funny thing is that I haven't taken a bubble bath in months and I haven't played a jazz record lately. This simple exercise has shown me at least two areas about myself that I almost forgot in the busyness of my daily routine.

It's also reminded me to appreciate some of my favorite people, places, and things a little more. My husband and my son are my favorite people in the whole world. It's a good feeling to put them in that perspective. And I think I'll get up early tomorrow and watch the sun rise. After all, early morning is my favorite time of day and I've forgotten to simply enjoy it for a while.

### Exercise #3

*What would I like to do?*

Next let's take a look at what you'd like to do if you had the time. If you were miraculously given the time, how would you:

Spend an extra hour each day?
Spend an extra day each week?

Spend an extra week each year?
Spend an extra year?

Don't think about all the things you *should* do with the extra time. Instead, think about those things you enjoy but just don't get around to. Don't worry about feeling guilty or being criticized or being responsible. This is *your* time to spend as you please. What would you do with it?

## Exercise #4

*What do others think of me?*

Next let's consider what others think of you, or what you *want* others to think of you. If you were being eulogized, what do you think friends and relatives would say about you? What would you most like to be remembered for? If your husband was asked to describe you, what do you think he would say? If your name came up in a conversation among friends, neighbors, or co-workers, what might they say about you?

Don't be too hard on yourself as you answer these questions. Most women have a tendency to be too critical; to see only their bad qualities and not their good. Think back on all the compliments you've received in your life and try to make a list of them. Don't discard those you don't believe, or those given by people whose sincerity you doubt.

This exercise may point up trouble spots as well as

unexpressed dreams. It should also point out strengths that others see in you that you may not admit to yourself.

## Exercise #5

*What can I do well?*

Take a look at the list of verbs on the following pages. Some of them describe specific skills. Others characterize types of behavior. Go through this list and

1. Place a check next to those that express something you *can* do.
2. Place a star next to the checked items you do *well.*
3. Circle those items with checks and stars that you especially enjoy doing.

| | | |
|---|---|---|
| Accounting | Assessing | Changing |
| Acting | Assigning | Classifying |
| Adapting | Assisting | Collaborating |
| Addressing | Balancing | Collecting |
| Administrating | Bargaining | Communicating |
| Advocating | Bookkeeping | Comparing |
| Allocating | Brainstorming | Compiling |
| Analyzing | Budgeting | Composing |
| Anticipating | Building | Computing |
| Appraising | Calculating | Conceptualizing |
| Arranging | Caring | Conducting |
| Assembling | Catering | Consulting |

| | | |
|---|---|---|
| Contributing | Enforcing | Investing |
| Controlling | Enlisting | Implementing |
| Cooking | Evaluating | Joking |
| Cooperating | Examining | Judging |
| Coordinating | Exercising | Knitting |
| Copying | Expediting | Leading |
| Counseling | Experimenting | Learning |
| Creating | Explaining | Lecturing |
| Critiquing | Expressing | Listening |
| Curing | Facilitating | Lobbying |
| Debating | Feeding | Managing |
| Decorating | Filing | Manipulating |
| Deciding | Fixing | Mapping |
| Defining | Forecasting | Mediating |
| Delivering | Fund raising | Memorizing |
| Delegating | Gardening | Modifying |
| Demonstrating | Gathering | Motivating |
| Designing | Graphing | Navigating |
| Detailing | Guiding | Needlepointing |
| Detecting | Hearing | Negotiating |
| Developing | Helping | Nursing |
| Diagnosing | Hostessing | Nurturing |
| Directing | Humoring | Observing |
| Discovering | Identifying | Operating |
| Discussing | Influencing | Ordering |
| Dissecting | Initiating | Organizing |
| Drawing | Innovating | Painting |
| Driving | Inspiring | Perceiving |
| Editing | Installing | Performing |
| Educating | Interpreting | Persevering |
| Encouraging | Inventing | Persuading |

| | | |
|---|---|---|
| Planning | Relaxing | Summarizing |
| Policy making | Remembering | Supervising |
| Preaching | Repairing | Supporting |
| Preparing | Reporting | Surveying |
| Prioritizing | Reproducing | Symbolizing |
| Processing | Researching | Systematizing |
| Programming | Restoring | Tabulating |
| Promoting | Reviewing | Talking |
| Problem solving | Risking | Teaching |
| Proofreading | Scanning | Team building |
| Proposing | Scheduling | Tending |
| Publicizing | Screening | Terminating |
| Public speaking | Self-motivating | Thinking |
| Purchasing | Selling | Training |
| Reacting | Servicing | Translating |
| Reading | Serving | Traveling |
| Reasoning | Shaping | Troubleshooting |
| Recommending | Simplifying | Typing |
| Reconciling | Singing | Understanding |
| Recording | Speaking | Updating |
| Recruiting | Staging | Validating |
| Reducing | Stimulating | Visualizing |
| Reflecting | Studying | Washing |
| Relating | Styling | Writing |

Now let's look at those skills that you've circled and expand on them. Write them below or on a separate sheet of paper and then list a more specific example of how you like to use that skill. For example, if you circled "listening" you might add, "to people who are troubled." If you circled "needlepointing," you might add "gifts for others."

*Skill          How I use it*

I hope this exercise has pointed the way toward recognizing the many skills you have. Whether you're a homemaker or a businesswoman, married or single, you have acquired certain skills so far in your life. What do you now know about yourself?

### Exercise #6

*What types of skills do I have?*

Next let's group your abilities by types to get a better idea of the kind of skills you are most interested in. Following are eight types of skills. List your circled verbs from the previous exercise under the areas that come closest to describing them.

*Artistic* (creative skills such as music, sewing, painting)

*Athletic* (hiking, playing tennis)

*Communications* (writing, speaking, translating)

*Educational* (teaching, guiding)

*Interpersonal* (advising, mediating, comforting)

*Manual* (typing, repairing)

*Organizational* (coordinating, managing)

*Persuasive* (promoting, selling)

Are you beginning to see some patterns emerge? In what area do you have the most skills? Is there any relationship between these skills and the types of activities you know you enjoy, such as the books you read, and so forth?

## Exercise #7

*What have I accomplished so far?*

Let's take a moment to replay the videotape of your life. Think of yourself at each stage of growth—as a child, adolescent, teenager, young adult—and where you are today. Think for a moment about what you enjoyed at each stage of life. What did you do well? What skills have you learned? What are your hobbies? What awards did you receive? What made you stand out in the crowd?

Make a list of the ten most important things you've accomplished in your life so far.

*My Most Important Accomplishments*

1.

2.

3.

4.

5.

6.

7.

8.

9.

10.

## Exercise #8

*What are the "givens"?*

Before we begin to match dreams with skills, it's important to take a hard look at reality. There are some things in your life that you cannot—or would not—change. They may be family obligations or physical handicaps or financial constraints. These are the "givens" of life; the elements we must learn to accept and the restrictions we must learn to live within. We all have circumstances that limit us in some way. Some of us are more limited than others. And during different stages of our lives we are more limited than at other times because of children or finances or careers.

It's important to look squarely at these limitations, accept them, and move on. Spending time on the "if only's" of life is an enormous waste of energy. We become very negative and bitter when we concentrate our attention on what we cannot do or be.

Think about the two women we met in the first chapter—Joni Eareckson Tada and Mary Crowley. Mary couldn't change the fact that the country was in a depression when she was looking for a way to support her family. She had two children and no husband—those were the facts of her situation. If she'd spent time feeling sorry for herself she would never have looked for a job or found a way to support her children. Today she might be a broken, bitter woman instead of a successful, happy woman who inspires others.

Whenever I begin to feel sorry for myself I think of

Joni Tada. It would be overwhelming to sit in a wheel-chair and think of all the "if only's." *If only I could walk. If only I could feed myself. If only I could pick a flower.* I'm sure that a person could literally go crazy if she found herself in a situation like Joni's and began to concentrate on all the things she could not do.

Yet Joni has accepted the givens and been willing to dream. She might not be able to walk, but she can sing. She might not be able to pick a flower, but she can paint one—by holding a paintbrush in her mouth. Some days I remind myself of all the things I have that Joni doesn't. And then I thank God for what He has given me. I think of the qualities Joni has that I need to develop—faith, courage, and the ability to accept reality while dreaming big dreams.

What are the "givens" in your life? They may not all be negative. They may be commitments you *wanted* to make or life-style decisions you believe in. But in some way they will define your life plan and direct you. List them below.

*The "Givens" in My Life*

At this point in my life my givens include a young son who requires my time and attention. I have financial obligations, including a mortgaged house and car payments. My husband and I have decided to make our home in a specific geographical location because of his job, our relatives, and the availability of good schools for our son.

I am fortunate to be in good health, have no overwhelming debt, and have a very supportive husband. When I think of the things I've achieved in my life, the skills I have, and my dreams for the future, I know that my givens are really not hindrances at all. I am thankful that they help define my path and limit my options.

What have you learned after listing the givens in your life? Aren't you thankful for the relatively few restrictions you have? Can you learn to accept them and actually thank God for them?

## The Next Step

Now that you have reviewed the videotape of your life and taken a closer look at where you are today, it's time to think about the next step. You have a list of dreams and a set of givens. You have hopes for the future and knowledge of current skills and past achievements. Take out your dream list again and read through everything you've listed.

Underline any dream that you could not pursue at this time because of the givens in your life. Be careful about this. Don't limit yourself unnecessarily. On the other hand, remember that these are dreams that may need to be postponed, but not necessarily forgotten. For example, one of my dreams is to live in Hawaii. Someday I really want to live there. But for the time being, a given in my life is to stay in the Washington, D.C., area. I am not abandoning this dream, but I am accepting the reality of my circumstances.

All of the dreams that you have underlined we'll call "someday" dreams. You probably won't see them come true this year or next, but five or ten years from now, when your circumstances have changed, who knows?

Next place a check mark next to all the dreams that would require resources, skills, or training beyond what you have today. My dream of being a ballerina falls into this category. I wouldn't even know how to begin to stand on my toes or twirl and jump. Furthermore, there's very little on my list of accomplishments from the past or my current skills that indicates I might have a natural talent in this area.

The dreams with check marks are long-term goals. They are things that you may be able to accomplish if you take classes or train or save enough money. You're probably not going to accomplish these this year, either. But you can at least start down the path toward achieving them.

Finally, circle all the dreams that you really could pursue over the next year. I really *could* lose ten pounds, learn to play a better game of tennis, buy that navy blue skirt, and even change my nose. It's all *possible.*

These are short-term goals. Some may seem crazy. Others seem quite achievable, given what you've done in the past and the skills you know you have. Don't worry about the fact that some are serious dreams and others are the kind you'd never even share with your closest friend.

Do you have dreams left over? I do. They include my wishes to meet a famous movie star and win a Pulitzer Prize. I really don't know if they're achievable, but they're fun dreams, what you might call fantasies. There's nothing wrong with having a category of dreams like these because they may be more possible than you realize. As you begin to make your dreams come true in the other areas, you may reassign your fantasies to "someday," "long-term," or "short-term" goals. As you make progress and begin to gain confidence in your ability to make your dreams come true, you'll realize how possible some of these fantasies really are.

*   *   *   *

Let's review some of the information you have learned about yourself in doing the preceding exercises.

1.  What did I learn about myself during each phase of life?
2.  What have I learned about myself by describing my current interests and favorite activities?

3. How would I spend an extra hour each day? An extra day each week? An extra week each year? An extra year?
4. What do I think others say about me? What are some of the compliments I've received?
5. What are the ten most important things I have accomplished so far?
6. What types of skills (artistic, athletic, etc.) do I primarily have?
7. What are the "givens" in my life?
8. What dreams could I pursue immediately, based on what I know about my skills, limitations, and interests? What dreams could I pursue with additional training, skills, or resources? What dreams will I have to set aside for now? What are my fun dreams? How could they become reality?

# 5. *What's Important to You?*

$A$ll of us who know Elizabeth discuss her with amazement and awe. Elizabeth is attractive, energetic, and talented. She's fascinated by the world around her and always excited about life. Unfortunately, Elizabeth is also the kind of person who may or may not show up for an appointment, rarely sticks with a job for more than a year, and is gung ho on a new project every time you see her. Her husband is a quiet, patient man whom we all describe as a saint.

Although I really enjoy Elizabeth I don't envy her. She is the kind of person who has potential but will probably do very little with it. Her energy is scattered and her priorities change every day. She has a hard time remembering what she values and because of that, often hurts others by forgetting commitments and ignoring obligations. Elizabeth is an unguided missile, zigzagging through life and never really going anywhere.

On the other hand, my friend Mary is a woman who has accomplished a great deal in her life already and will probably continue to do great things. She's raised five wonderful children and now works at an exciting job. She began as a secretary and did such excellent work that she kept getting promoted. Although she's not beautiful, almost everyone describes her as being attractive—she's thin and wears fashionable clothes, which she makes herself. A superwoman? Not really. She's an ordinary woman who concentrates her energy on what is important at the time. Mary knows the value of establishing priorities and sticking with them.

Whether you have formally established it or not, you do have a set of priorities. Where you spend your time and energy shows your current priorities and points out what you value. For many of us, what we say is most important is not necessarily what we demonstrate to those around us. We all know people who say their family is important to them yet seem to do everything possible to spend their time working or engaged in activities that take them away from home.

A few years ago I was in church when the pastor read Matthew 6:33: "Seek ye first the kingdom of God, and his righteousness; and all these things shall be added unto you."

"Do you put God first in your life?" the pastor asked. *Of course,* I mentally affirmed. As a Christian I was committed to placing God first on my priority list. But the minister didn't stop there. He began to ask how we spent our time each day, what we did when we had time to spare, what we daydreamed about. When he was finished, I realized that I might have been saying that God was my most important priority, but in fact He was barely in the top ten. I realized then that I had to face up to the fact that I was saying one thing and living another.

What's really important to you? What do you value? You may get an idea by looking at the things you've already done with your life and the type of dreams you've listed.

Take a look at the list below and consider who and what are important to you. Be honest. You don't have to tell anyone your answers, but it is important to take time to think about them.

*I Value:*

| | |
|---|---|
| Marriage | Faith |
| Parents | Beauty |
| Children | Health |
| Home | Honesty |
| Work | Independence |
| Friends | Education |
| Money | Pleasure |
| Power | Security |

| | |
|---|---|
| Wisdom | Freedom |
| Pets | Peace |
| Youth | Competence |
| Intelligence | Other: _____ |
| Fitness | _____ |

Go down the list and number each in terms of its importance to you, from most important to least important. Now list below the five most important values in your life:

1.
2.
3.
4.
5.

Let's try another method of clarifying values. If you knew you had only six months to live, how would you spend your time? Use a separate sheet of paper and spend ten minutes listing all the things you would do during the six months.

When you have finished your list, compare the things you would do with what you are actually doing now. Is there a great discrepancy between what you would do if you were running out of time versus the way you live your life today? What is preventing you from doing those things?

If I had only six months to live, I'd want to see all my friends and relatives to say good-bye and spend time with my immediate family. The fact that I would spend time with my family reminds me that they are important enough to me so that I should make them a top priority *now* when I plan my time. And, although at this point I wouldn't quit my job and fly all over the country to see my friends, I am reminded that it's important to stay in touch by telephone or through letters. I need to be better about communicating with my friends and letting them know how important they are to me.

What can you learn about yourself from this hypothetical question that will help you live the next six months in a manner consistent with your true priorities?

Let's go back to the five things you value. On the following page you'll see a chart that will help you put your values together with your dreams. List your five top priorities down the left side of the chart. Then take out your dream list and begin to list your short-term dreams next to the priority to which it relates. Think through the underlying desires for your dreams as you list them. For example, one of my top priorities is my marriage. I've placed my short-term dream of losing weight and firming muscles next to "marriage" because I want to do both to be more attractive for my husband. My dream of having that navy blue skirt goes next to "work." I imagine myself looking very professional in that skirt and that's really why I want it.

You'll notice that following the places for your five priorities there's a sixth block of space. This is the spot to place all those dreams that will help *you* grow personally. You may not have placed yourself in your top five priorities, but it is important that you continue to grow and stretch as a person.

Once you've listed your short-term dreams, do the same for your long-term, and then for those someday dreams. If you run out of space, copy this form onto another sheet of paper.

| Priorities | Short-term dreams | Long-term dreams | Someday dreams |
|---|---|---|---|
| 1. ____ | | | |
| 2. ____ | | | |
| 3. ____ | | | |
| 4. ____ | | | |
| 5. ____ | | | |

Using this chart, we'll begin to set goals, the first step in developing a life plan.

What do you see as you begin to place your dreams next to your values? Perhaps you notice that many of your dreams simply don't fit your value system. Could that be because the things you *say* you value aren't really most important to you? Or are the "givens" in your life helping you define realistic goals?

When my friend Janice discusses her dreams, she usually includes some expensive hobbies like flying her own plane and traveling around the world. She considers "money" a top priority. When I challenged her recently to define those dreams in terms of her values, she hesitated. Janice works at a low-paying job and doesn't consider work high on her priority list. But if she is ever going to make her dreams come true, she is going to have to make more money (or inherit a fortune).

The hard reality of the situation forced Janice to take another look at her values. If she really wanted to make her dreams come true, she'd have to work harder to improve her income or she'd have to find another way to learn to fly and travel. Janice finally decided that she really didn't care that much about expensive pastimes; she was simply dreaming about ways to escape from her boring job. Soon after our discussion she began applying for positions with airlines. She understands now that "money" wasn't a real value. Instead, she valued freedom and saw money as a way of achieving freedom.

### Turning dreams into goals

By now you probably suspect that your dream list is being shaped into a list of goals. Dreams are ideas or ambitions that you think about, but goals are meant to be pursued. In order to turn a dream into a goal, you have to ask yourself these five questions:

1. Is it specific?
2. How will I know I have achieved it?
3. Do I know the cost in terms of time and resources?
4. Am I willing to pay that price?

5.   Will I be living consistently with my values if I
     achieve this?

Let's walk through two of my short-term dreams and
see if they can be goals. The first is my desire to lose
weight. In order to make it specific I need to come up
with the number of pounds I want to lose—ten. It may
sound obvious to say I'll know I've achieved it when
the scale reads "120," but I tend to avoid weighing myself, so I'll have to begin doing so on a regular basis.

I know the cost of losing that weight is no more desserts, butter, or gravy for at least two months. More
specifically, I know that if I restrict my calorie intake to
1,200 calories a day, I can lose two pounds a week at
first and a pound a week later. That means that I can
shed my extra weight in six to eight weeks. Watching
my diet for about two months is the cost.

Am I willing to do it? I've said so before, but this
time I'm willing to make a commitment. It's really a
small price to pay for a slender me.

If I do lose weight, I will be living more consistently
with my values. I know that as a Christian my body is
the temple of God. I know that my husband will be
pleased with a slimmer wife. I will be healthier. And I
will probably be a better mother if I feel better about
myself. *I'll do it.*

Now let's look at another short-term dream—a new
nose. I want a new nose because I think mine is too big.
What I really want is a cute little turned-up nose. I'll
know I've achieved it when I recover from plastic sur-
gery and look in the mirror. It's going to cost money—I

hear about $3,000. It's going to be painful. And it's going to take about a week of time away from work.

I'm not really willing to pay that price. I guess my nose isn't *that* bad. My husband thinks it's a crazy idea; I have to believe God created me this way; and it's not likely I'll be a better person because of a new nose. In fact, maybe I've developed a depth of character I wouldn't have if my nose were perfect. That does it. I've talked myself right out of a nose job.

It may seem time consuming, but walking yourself through this exercise for each of your dreams is important. You begin to make decisions about what you *really* want, which will help you commit yourself to making your dreams come true. And you will discover that some of your dreams will never become actual goals. They're either too costly or inconsistent with your values. They're not worth the time or energy necessary to achieve them.

You will also discover that you should be able to answer these questions specifically for short-term dreams, but long-term and someday dreams will be more difficult to measure in terms of cost. That's fine at this point. You may be able to eliminate some longer-term dreams because you see that they are inconsistent with your values. But don't be too quick to eliminate them because you're unwilling to pay the price of achieving them. Remember that your life may be different five years from now. Your children may be growing, giving you more time to pursue other interests. As family finances change, you may not need to work outside the home. Many things can and will change in the future.

After going through this exercise you have probably abandoned some dreams altogether and turned others into goals. Use a sheet of paper or the chart provided to list your goals under each priority area. Take the time to list your goals neatly and make your chart readable. This is your first step in developing a life plan.

| Priorities | Short-term goals | Long-term goals | Someday goals |
|---|---|---|---|
| 1. | | | |
| 2. | | | |
| 3. | | | |
| 4. | | | |
| 5. | | | |

\*     \*     \*     \*

Remember the importance of determining true priorities in making your dreams come true.

1. What do you really value?
2. What are the five most important values in your life?
3. If you had only six months to live, how would you spend your time? How would you live differently from the way you live now?
4. What do your dreams tell you about your true values?

5. As you turn your dreams into goals, remember to ask:

Is it specific?
How will I know I have achieved it?
Do I know the cost?
Am I willing to pay the price?
Will I be living consistently with my values
   if I achieve this?

# 6. *Making Your Dreams Come True*

A few years ago my friend Ann and her husband moved into a "handyman's special" house that looked as if it were on the verge of being condemned. The first time I visited Ann I was horrified by the condition of the house, yet she was smiling as she described its potential. Knowing that Ann was pregnant and her husband was in a job that paid very little, I wondered how she was ever going to make the house habitable.

It took her six years to do it, but Ann and her husband, Chuck, now live in a house that is truly breath-taking. The floors have been sanded and refinished. The walls are patched and painted. A beautiful hand-made quilt hangs in the entrance. And the windows are framed by drapes Ann made herself.

How did she do it? She didn't have much money, but she did have time and energy and she was committed to making the house a home for her family. Ann started by going to model homes in new developments to see what decorating tips she could learn. She studied *Architectural Digest* at the local library (she didn't have enough money to subscribe). She asked people whose homes she admired for tips and suggestions.

Then she made a list of all the things that needed to be done in her house, the cost of each improvement, and the amount of time each would take. She started with the "easy" things like painting walls. In her spare time she worked on the quilt, which took her two years to complete. She pinched pennies in cooking and her wardrobe so she could buy fabric (at a discount store) for drapes. And she even traded baby-sitting services for the wallpapering expertise of a neighbor.

Ann's house wasn't transformed overnight. It took hard work, determination—and planning. Ann set her sights on a goal, took the time to understand what the cost was, and then went after it. And she achieved what most people would have considered impossible.

When I first read the *Autobiography of Benjamin Franklin,* I was amazed by the fact that this great man had struggled with some very common personality flaws. Thinking about all his accomplishments, I had always assumed that he was just born with more talents and abilities than most people. Yet in his autobiography Franklin describes his plan for overcoming such problems as pride and insincerity, and becoming a better man.

Franklin carefully listed thirteen character traits he wished to improve. Then he marked each day of the week across the top of seven columns. Each week Franklin concentrated his efforts on overcoming one bad habit, but also checked the other habits he was trying to overcome. At the end of thirteen weeks he began to see progress. But his goal was to completely overcome all of his bad habits. Instead of just congratulating himself he went back and repeated the process over and over again until he integrated his new habits into his daily life.

If there is one thing I've learned about myself over the years, it's that I need a plan if I want to make big things happen in my life. Sometimes I'm lucky and good things come my way. Sometimes I'm less fortunate. But if I don't have a plan, my life is controlled by external circumstances. Without a plan Ann would still be living in a broken-down house. Without a plan Benjamin Franklin might have been an eccentric, forgotten man instead of an American statesman.

A plan is a way of getting you from point A to point B. It shows you how to take those dreams that have now become goals and make them into accomplishments. A plan gives you a road map to trace; an agenda to follow; an instruction manual to implement. It's what keeps you going when you want to give up and what keeps you on track when you're tempted to get caught up in some new activity.

How do you develop a plan? You're well on your way since you've already learned to dream, assess your skills and values, and prioritize your goals. Now it's time for *action.*

### Your personal plan

Remember that everyone has different dreams, skills, values, and goals; therefore, everyone will have a very different plan. These steps are designed to help you accomplish what *you* really want. They're just a method to help you organize your thinking and direct your energies.

### 1. *Establish your priorities.*

You may have three goals in each of your six value categories to work on short-term and several more long-term goals. How do you keep them all going at once? Unless you're unusually gifted and disciplined, you probably won't be able to concentrate on more than three to five goals at any given time. You need to look through your goals and prioritize them. Try to decide which are really the most important goals you could begin to pursue. What would make the greatest difference in your life? What would *really* make you happy?

Take out another sheet of paper and write at the top, "The Most Important Goals in My Life Are:" and then list them below.

### 2. *Be specific.*

As you analyzed each of your dreams, you saw the importance of being specific about what you wanted. It isn't enough to say you want to lose weight; you need to decide exactly how much you'll lose. I emphasize this again, because I think it's one of the biggest mistakes people make when they begin to develop a plan. They fail to take the time to develop very specific goals, ones that can be established and measured.

Go through your goals and try to find ways to make them even more specific. Even longer-term goals should be as specific as possible. If a long-term goal of yours is to have a happy marriage, try to envision exactly what you mean by that. Talk to your husband about what he would consider the key ingredients in a happy marriage. Look at other marriages and discover what you like and don't like about them. Does a happy marriage mean that you and your husband would never fight? Does it mean you would spend more time together? Does it mean you would go away for romantic weekends each year?

If you don't know what you specifically want, you'll have a hard time developing a plan to achieve your goals. You may become frustrated because you don't have a clear picture of your target.

### 3. *Brainstorm.*

For every goal you establish, there are any number of routes by which to achieve it. By spending time brainstorming about the ways to achieve your goal, you explore the various routes and consider your options. This exercise is important for two reasons. First, you begin to envision how you're actually going to achieve your goal, and second, you establish contingency plans in case your first approach doesn't work.

I find it helpful to brainstorm on paper, so I take a sheet of paper for each of my goals and write the goal across the top. Then under the goal I write all the possible ways I might achieve it.

For example, in order to lose weight I can:

> count calories
> follow the Scarsdale Diet
> go to a health spa
> fast
> exercise, but eat normally
> take up running

In order to have a better marriage I can:

> spend more time alone with my husband
> learn more about his work
> remember to compliment him
> keep the house neater
> read books on marriage

help with the financial planning
stop interrupting my husband

You can see that brainstorming helps develop alternatives as well as specific components in a plan. In the first example, I was looking at different courses I could follow, while for the second goal I was listing elements which may all become part of my plan.

You will notice, too, that brainstorming should help you explore all of the options for achieving your goal, from the obvious to the idealistic.

## 4.   *Gather information.*

I may have a wonderful list of possible ways to pursue my goal, but I still need to gather information. For example, is it realistic to expect that I can go to a health spa to lose weight? I need to find out how much it costs to go to one and how many pounds a person can lose at a spa. Can running help me lose weight? I'm sure it can, but how much would I have to run each week in order to lose ten pounds? I've heard people say that the Scarsdale Diet is a great way to lose weight, but what exactly is the diet? Do I have to commit myself to eating foods I dislike? Is it medically safe?

The information-gathering stage is a time to sift through the alternative paths and begin to make some decisions about the course you'll want to take. It's a time to evaluate options in terms of cost, time, and energy commitment.

5. *Prioritize.*

After gathering information I'm ready to list my options in order of priority. For my weight-loss goal I've decided to follow a balanced diet, but reduce my calorie intake. I've also decided to try to burn 300 calories a day through some form of exercise.

Fasting is an alternative I place low on the list because after reading what experts say, I'm not sure it's a healthy way to diet. The health spa is down the list, too, because I discovered that the price tag of $1,000 to $3,000 for a week was more than I was willing to spend.

For my marriage goal I've decided to read one book on marriage right away and begin to keep the house neater, since I know it will immediately make my husband happier. Next on my list is the need to stop interrupting my husband while he's talking. Further down the list is helping with the financial planning.

6. *Develop a plan.*

For each goal you have decided to pursue you need to establish a written plan. Copy the form below on to another sheet of paper and use it for each of your goals.

Goal: _____

Target date: _____

How I'm going to do it:

    1.

    2.

3.

4.

5.

What I will feel like when I've accomplished it: \_\_\_\_

_____

I need help from:_____

I am pursuing this goal because: _____

_____

Write down your goal in clear, precise language. Then look at your calendar and decide on an *exact* date by which you hope to achieve your goal. For long-term goals, this may be difficult, so (1) set a date by which you will evaluate your progress toward your goal and (2) break your long-term goals into short-term projects.

Obviously, the goal of having a better marriage isn't something I can decide to achieve by a certain date. But on the first Saturday of each month I will evaluate my progress and by that date I will try to accomplish certain things, such as reading a book, becoming neater, and waiting until my husband finishes his sentence before I begin to speak.

Are you going to accomplish your goal alone? Probably not. At least with most goals you'll need the direct help or moral support of someone else. I need my husband to help me lose weight and to help us have a good marriage. And I need to pray for the strength to stick to my diet and for the ability to keep from interrupting my husband.

Finally, why are you pursuing this goal? This relates your goal back to the values you established earlier as well as other emotions that go into your thinking. You may be pursuing a goal because you believe it is right, based on your values. You may be pursuing it because it's a dream you always had and want badly enough to work at making it come true. Perhaps you know that reaching your goal will simply make you happy or you believe it will make you feel better about yourself. List as many of these reasons as you can for each goal. Whenever your commitment wavers, refer back to the ultimate reasoning behind your decision.

### 7.  *Commit yourself.*

Just by going this far in establishing a plan, you will have developed a certain degree of commitment to each of your goals. But in order to achieve each goal you have to make trade-offs. I will have to give up desserts and find time to read books on marriage. It won't be easy to do either of these things. But I know, in order to reach my goals, it's important for me to pay the price.

Once you've really decided to achieve a goal you may want to enlist someone who can help you stick to your commitment. Don't tell everyone you know that you're on a diet or that you're trying to improve your marriage. But, if appropriate, share your goal with your husband or a close friend who can help you keep on track.

Then you'll want to pray about your commitment. God can give you the power to realize your dreams and help you be all you can be. By asking Him for the strength to achieve your goal, you are also affirming that you can "do all things through Christ" (*see* Philippians 4:13).

### 8. *Reinforce your commitment.*

Every morning when you wake up, review your goals and mentally affirm them. Write your goals down on a 3 × 5 card and place it in your purse. Whenever you have a minute, while waiting for an appointment or even while you're in line at the checkout counter, reread your goals and commit yourself to them.

Cut pictures out of magazines that remind you of the results of achieving your goal. (I cut out a picture of a skinny model and of a happy couple.) Tape those pictures to your mirror and every time you look at yourself think of what will happen in the future as a result of achieving your goal.

### 9. *Learn from your failures.*

Just because you've committed yourself to a goal doesn't mean you'll never succumb to temptation. It happens from time to time to all of us. But it's important that a small failure does not cause you to abandon your goal altogether. If you give in to a piece of chocolate cake, you don't have to give up on the diet. Go back to it tomorrow and remind yourself that chocolate is an especially difficult temptation, so you'll need to avoid it altogether.

Don't condemn yourself for failure. You'll only convince yourself that you will never live up to the goal you've established. Instead face up to it: "I ate one piece of chocolate cake today which was *not* on my diet." Then remind yourself of what you've done right so far: "This is the first time in a week that I haven't followed my diet." Next, put it in perspective: "I have two months to reach my desired weight and I can still do it if I go back to my diet and stick with it." Then review your ultimate reasoning for establishing the goal and envision yourself succeeding once again.

### 10. *Reward yourself.*

Plan something special for yourself when you reach your goal. If you've been dieting, look forward to splurging on a brand-new pair of size 8 slacks. Or plan a special dinner with your husband when you've made progress toward a marriage goal. Remember to concentrate on the positive reward you'll receive, every time you're tempted by a momentary diversion that will slow your progress toward your ultimate goal.

Set intermediate rewards too. If it will take you more than a month to achieve your goal, you'll probably need some intermediate incentives. The rewards don't have to be expensive. Buy yourself a rose or treat yourself to an entire morning of guilt-free relaxation. Go for a walk in the park or visit a tourist sight in your town. Whatever you do, make it special, anticipate it, and give yourself the reward as a token of belief in your ability to set a goal and achieve it.

\*   \*   \*   \*

Review these questions while working on your goals.

1.  What are three to five goals you could pursue today that would make the greatest difference in your life?
2.  What *exactly* do you want to achieve?
3.  What are all the ways you can achieve each goal?
4.  What is the cost of achieving each goal?
5.  What is the best path to choose toward achieving each goal?
6.  What will you feel like when you've accomplished each goal?
7.  Who can help you pursue your goals?
8.  Why are you pursuing each goal?
9.  How can you reinforce your commitment?
10. What reward will you promise yourself for achieving each goal?

# 7. *Finding the Time*

It may feel wonderful to dream big dreams and set exciting goals, but ultimately you will probably ask, "Where in the world will I find the time?" If you're like most of us, you already feel pulled in too many directions. How can you find extra hours to pursue those five important goals when there are dinners to cook and reports to type and clothes to wash?

Although King Solomon asked for the gift of wisdom, I bet that given the choice many of us would ask for more time. But even with forty-eight hours in every day, would we really have all the time necessary? Probably not. I suspect that I'd make the same mistakes with forty-eight hours that I do with twenty-four hours—and probably end up twice as frustrated.

I once read that you can always find time for the most important things. The fact is that the way you spend your time now shows what is most important to you. You need to readjust your hours to be consistent with your values and your priorities. You need to find ways to devote your time to the essentials.

There are literally dozens of time-management books, tapes, and seminars on the market to help you get control of your hours. Many of them are excellent and most of them can give you important basic principles to follow. But I've found that most of the books I've read on time management are written for busy executives who have secretaries to screen calls and the ability to shut their doors while they work on important projects.

Most women lead a very different kind of life. Whether you're a full-time homemaker or a career woman and a homemaker, you know that your daily schedule may be subject to the whims of half a dozen other people. In fact, I've found that most women, whether married or single, career or home oriented, share the same frustrations in managing their time. These problems include:

1. *Planning ahead.* Buying groceries for the week is a great idea, but when your husband announces that he'll be out of town for the next two nights or your son brings a few friends home for dinner, your planning goes out the window. Single women may find that spur-of-the-moment activities and dates are fun but make planning difficult. Women's liberation or not, women still find themselves responding to others much of the time.

2. *Defining roles.* I am a boss, cook, manager, mother, editor, diaper changer, writer, gardener.... It's hard for me to keep track of all the roles I play each day. Because of that I have a hard time "shifting gears" from one role to the next. When I'm at work, I need to be organized, professional, and decisive. When I'm with my son I need to slow my pace, stop worrying about spills and messes, and be flexible enough to laugh one minute and reprimand the next. It's totally appropriate for me to try to schedule as many activities as possible at work, but while with my son I need just to be with him and enjoy him.

3. *Delegating.* For some reason women have a difficult time delegating work to others. "Oh, it's easier if I just do it myself" is the standard line most of us use when someone suggests we pass a job along. The majority of us have very little experience delegating in the first place. Who would we delegate to, even if we were willing? It's not as though most of us have a household staff ready to repond to our call. And if we did delegate the work, would it be done well enough to suit our standards? Wouldn't it cost more than we'd be willing to pay? Women tend to undervalue their personal time and to find the idea of using others to do their work very intimidating.

### Principles of Time Management for Women

Given these basic problems, how can women learn to use their time more efficiently? Let's consider ten principles that can put more hours in your day. They're not particularly new principles, but they are explained with a woman's needs in mind.

1. *Simplify your life.* When I first got married, I was most surprised by my husband's closet. His clothes only took up half a rack and his three pairs of shoes were placed neatly on the floor. All the rest of his clothes fit into a small dresser. He had all his toiletries on two shelves of a medicine cabinet.

While we were dating, I had always thought of Tom as a well-dressed person. I never noticed him wearing the same clothes over and over or dressing inappropriately for any occasion. But I was astounded to think that all his possessions took up so little room.

I think he may have wished he'd never asked me to marry him when I began moving the boxes and boxes of my possessions into his apartment. I come from a family of savers, and many of the things I was moving in were items that I held on to "just in case" I'd need them someday.

Although Tom was always good-natured about it, it became apparent during our early years of marriage that my belongings took up three-quarters of our apartment. And for some reason I was the one who never had anything to wear or needed to run to the drugstore at midnight because I was out of shampoo.

Slowly, Tom's way of life seemed to make sense to me. I began to give away clothes I didn't wear and discard my collection of nearly used-up lipsticks. I began to sort through magazines each month and clear the coffee table of old issues. Tom never forced me to clean up my act, but once I started down the path of clutter-free living, I became addicted. It was so much easier to find clothes to wear in the morning. I stopped losing bills and I could see when I was down to my last bottle of shampoo. Although I'm not completely reformed, I do know that every step I take toward simplifying my life gives me more time and helps me make everyday decisions more quickly. The principles I've used to simplify my life are elementary, but perhaps they'll help you move toward clutter-free living.

Before buying anything, ask yourself:

Do I really need this?
How often will I use it?
What do I already own that I could use instead?
Is it worth the space it will take up?
Will I have to buy anything else to go with it?

Once a month go through each room of the house looking for:

Anything that can be thrown out
Anything not used that can be stored or given
  away
Anything seasonal that should be put away
Anything that doesn't serve a purpose anymore

Go through every drawer and closet every six months looking for items that fit the categories above.

As much as possible, rent (or borrow) instead of buying items you won't use more than once a year. Don't buy anything that's really "in" this season—including clothing and the latest appliances. Give yourself a few months to decide if you really need it. (Chances are the price will be lower anyway, if you really do decide to buy it in a few months.)

2. *Organize everything.* My rule is that if there's more than one of them or it happens more than once every six months, I need some form of organization to deal with it. Organizing things helps me make fewer decisions. I decided *once* that bills go in a bin marked "bills" which is on my desk. I never again worry about where to put them so I don't forget to pay them. All of my baking ingredients (flour, baking soda, brown sugar, etc.) go in one cupboard. My husband can help me put away groceries because my system makes sense to him.

I'm not naturally organized and neither are most people. But *I am* naturally lazy and I have found that getting things organized ultimately takes less time and energy than dealing with chaos every day. Files, bins, and drawer dividers are inexpensive ways to help me find more time for the important things in life.

3. *Keep a list of ten-minute jobs.* I have typed up a list of daily tasks that take ten minutes or less and I keep copies of the list in my purse and on my bulletin board in the kitchen. I have a separate list of ten-minute jobs for my office. Here are some of the items that appear on my home list:

Empty the dishwasher
Water the plants
Dust one room
Polish two pairs of shoes

Sort through the magazines on the coffee table
Iron a shirt
Write a postcard
Sew a button on a skirt
Clean out my pocketbook

It's amazing how many things can be accomplished in ten minutes. And it's also amazing how many times during the day you find yourself with ten minutes to spare. My ten-minute accomplishments give me such a good feeling that I usually do at least one each day. Those annoying little jobs that mount up can also disappear quickly when you attack them one at a time.

4. *Do more than one thing at a time.* Most of us do more than one thing at a time because of necessity, but it helps to plan to batch activities together. For example, if you spend much time on the phone, you might want to keep your sewing kit in a nearby drawer so you can take care of repairs while talking. Or you might even keep your exercise bicycle within reach of the telephone so you can work out while chatting. Some women iron while watching TV or cook while listening to foreign-language tapes. It doesn't matter what you do, but it does help to plan ahead to accomplish as much as possible.

Make a list of all the things you can do at the same time. Then be sure you get set up to take advantage of the opportunities.

5. *Eliminate time wasters.* Every one of us wastes time each day, whether we realize it or not. One of the best ways to become a better time manager is to keep a

time log for a week on which you note everything you do by half-hour intervals. I know it sounds tedious, but it is absolutely the only way to discover all the ways time seems to evaporate into thin air. Copy the time form below and use it to keep track of your days for the next week. Don't try to do anything unusual. And remember that there's no such thing as an ordinary week. At the end of the week add up the time spent on various activities such as personal grooming, talking on the telephone, watching television, preparing meals, commuting, and so forth. Could you possibly cut back the time you spend on any area?

When I did my time log, I was shocked by the results. Although I typically say that I "never watch TV," I discovered that I'd spent nearly fifteen hours in front of the television set and only two hours reading. I also realized that several blocks of time were interrupted by telephone calls from salespeople.

## Time Log

6:00

6:30

7:00

7:30

8:00

8:30

9:00

9:30

10:00

10:30

11:00

11:30

12:00

12:30

1:00

1:30

2:00

2:30

3:00

3:30

4:00

4:30

5:00

5:30

6:00

6:30

7:00

7:30

8:00

8:30

9:00

9:30

10:00

10:30

11:00

11:30

12:00

I cut back my television viewing and restricted myself to certain television shows. Then I was able to begin reading more books. My husband and I also decided to buy a telephone-answering machine, because it seemed that the telephone was always ringing while we were busy with the baby. The answering machine turned out to be such a time-saver that we use it all the time now. We can leave it on when we're busy and return calls when we're finished. We can also leave messages for each other if we're both away from the house.

Before I did my time log, I probably would have imagined that my time wasters were very different than they turned out to be. Now I use a time log every few months just to take another look at my schedule and to see what new time wasters have crept in.

6. *Keep monthly, weekly, and daily project lists.* I've heard a lot of people laugh at "to do" lists, but I couldn't live without mine. I start with a list of all the things I want to accomplish for the month. This list has either my major goals or a project for my major goals on it. This month's list included:

> Finish book
> Lose five pounds
> Read a marriage book
> Find extra time to be with the baby
> Repair winter clothes and store away
> Plan surprise shower for friends
> Get tickets for vacation

Next to each project I try to estimate how many hours it will take. Then I begin to assign parts of each project to each week of the month. At the beginning of each week I write a note to myself: "By _____ (date of the last day of the week) I will . . ."

My weekly list might read:

Write chapters 7 & 8
Go to exercise class at lunch
Read chapters 1–4 of marriage book
Come home early on Tuesday and Thursday
   to be with baby
Check all wool skirts for repairs
Purchase invitations
Call travel agent

Once again, I will place a time estimate next to each item.

Finally, I will take items from my weekly list and place them on my daily list. Then I will schedule my time around these activities, leaving plenty of time for unexpected interruptions.

At the end of each month I go back to make sure I've accomplished everything on my list. If not, I add it to next month's list and repeat the procedure. By going through this exercise I am able to accomplish twice as much as I once did. And, although I sometimes have to take care of things I'd rather not do at the time, I find that I do have more flexibility in my schedule because I can always rearrange my projects if necessary.

7. *Prioritize.* Always do the most important things first, and you'll accomplish more than you ever imagined you could. It sounds obvious, but most of us do just the opposite. We do the easy things or the least

important, putting off the most important until we're tired or less alert. My theory is that when I have an important project to complete, I let it intimidate me. I think about it, worry about it, and then put it off until it becomes bigger than life. I've learned, though, that if I attack the important projects first thing in the morning, when I'm well-rested and energetic, I can usually accomplish them fairly quickly. I'm often surprised by how easy it is to do something important when I approach it first thing in the morning.

There are different ways to prioritize your projects, but I use an A, B, C system. Next to my monthly, weekly, and daily goals I place a letter indicating its importance. A's absolutely, positively must get done. B's better get done, or I'll have to take care of them later. C's should get done, but I probably won't be in big trouble if they slide. When I finish my A's I go to my B's and then to my C's. It's really that simple.

8. *Be realistic.* Don't try to be a superwoman when you make your project lists. Allow plenty of time to accomplish each task. Leave lots of extra time in your schedule for interruptions. Don't try to schedule yourself too optimistically or you'll find yourself frustrated.

For example, on days I'm at home I estimate that I can get a total of three hours worth of projects completed. Because my son is totally unpredictable, I can't schedule more than that because he might be having one of his days when he needs attention and takes two short naps. I plan to work during his two half-hour naps, while he plays alone during two half-hour periods, and for an hour in the evening while my husband watches him. In those three hours I can accomplish a great deal. And often I actually get four or five hours instead of three. Those days are a nice surprise, but I don't plan on them. I'd only be frustrated by what I didn't accomplish if I did. Instead I plan for three hours (in half-hour segments) and usually feel confident that my project list will be completed by the end of the day.

9. *Break larger projects into smaller tasks.* It's easy to become overwhelmed by a large project and the amount of time it will take to accomplish it. But every large job can be broken down into smaller, more approachable tasks. And then every task can be accomplished in a reasonable amount of time.

The thought of writing a book was overwhelming to me. I had no idea how long it would take to research, write, edit, and rewrite such a large volume of material. The longest article I'd ever written was about the length of one chapter in a book, and I knew I'd need to write at least ten times that amount to finish a book-length manuscript.

After I signed a contract, I spent almost a month worrying and considering my options. Should I quit work and devote myself to writing full-time? Should I get up at 4:00 A.M. every morning and write until I went to work? Should I spend every weekend for a year writing? Should I simply admit that I'd made a mistake and cancel the book?

None of these options sounded very promising, so I decided to try to get a better idea of what I needed to do. I spent one hour calling people I knew who had written books and asking them how long it took. Their answers ranged from forty hours to three years. (I began to get very worried!) Finally I decided to deal with the facts as I knew them. I knew that in order to write a 3,000-word article (about the length of a book chapter) it typically took me eight hours of research, six hours of writing, and an hour of editing before it was ready to be typed. Since I thought a book chapter might be more difficult, I decided to double those estimates, which meant each chapter of a book would take me thirty hours to write. If the book was going to be ten chapters, I would need to spend about 300 hours writing.

That made the project a little more approachable. I knew that I needed to spend six hours a week for the next year on writing the book. I could do it by spending an hour each day, or giving up a good portion of my Saturdays for the coming year.

Next I made a comprehensive outline of the whole book and tried to outline each chapter. That made me realize that each chapter would have smaller portions, which I could write in shorter periods of time.

Suddenly I was feeling better about the whole project. I knew that I could write the pieces that added up to a chapter. And ten of those chapters added up to a book! As long as I concentrated on the smaller tasks and didn't get overwhelmed by the magnitude of the project, it seemed very approachable.

The steps I followed to write this book are the same ones you can use to attack any large project—whether it's starting a garden or having a dinner party. Just re-member to keep breaking those big jobs into smaller tasks and than tackle them one by one.

10. *Always make a daily schedule.* Every day, no matter how busy you are, sit down for five minutes and schedule your day on a 3 × 5 card. List all the times when you know certain things will occur. Write down all appointments that you've already planned and the length of time they'll take.

After you list the scheduled activities, begin to write in your most important projects. Schedule half an hour for unexpected interruptions in both the morning and afternoon. (If you have small children, you'll need to schedule more time here.) Give yourself a block of time to make phone calls.

Then take your day's schedule, review it, and forget about everything else you have to do tomorrow. Just concentrate on the projects you have scheduled for today. Carry your schedule wherever you go. Make a game of trying to stick to it.

I can tell you from my own experience that schedul-ing your day and sticking to it will help you get more done than you ever imagined.

\*     \*     \*     \*

These time-management principles are just a way to get you started. Read other books on the subject and ask your friends for their tips. Become a collector of time-saver ideas. Remember, on a regular basis, to ask yourself:

1. How can I simplify my life?
2. What can I organize to help me make fewer decisions and avoid clutter?
3. What jobs can I accomplish in ten minutes?
4. Can I do more than one thing at a time? How can I get organized to take advantage of those times?
5. How do I waste time?
6. What projects do I need to work on this month? This week? Each day?
7. What is the most important thing I have to accomplish?
8. What can I *realistically* do today?
9. How can I break my larger projects into smaller tasks?
10. What can I learn from scheduling each day?

# 8. *Gaining Control*

I hadn't seen Beth for weeks, so when we met for lunch one day we spent some breathless minutes catching up on the latest news. By the time the waiter came to take our order, we hadn't even opened the menu. But it didn't really matter. "Just give me a small garden salad with oil and vinegar dressing on the side," Beth said. I took the same and as the waiter left we both began to giggle. "Still dieting?" she asked.

"Of course," I replied. "I'll be dieting for the rest of my life." The battle of the waistlines was just one of the many things Beth and I shared. We both loved to eat and hated what happened to us when we indulged.

After finishing our salads, Beth and I were feeling very smug. But when the waiter came along and began to describe the special chocolate cheesecake for dessert, we both began to weaken. "I will if you will" was the only encouragement we needed. Before we knew it, our low-calorie lunch had turned into a disaster. We both gave a guilty groan as we laid down our forks after consuming the last morsels of the calorie-laden cheesecake.

"You know, I really mean to watch my diet," Beth said. "But somehow I just don't have the discipline. Why is it that I can't control myself, even when I hate myself afterwards?"

Beth's words summed up my feelings, too. I've found that lack of discipline is one of the greatest obstacles to turning dreams into accomplishments. Even when we find the time to take steps toward those carefully planned goals, we often lack the discipline to really make things happen.

Actually I've never known anyone who matter-of-factly said, "Discipline is no problem for me." It seems that in one way or another we all struggle to control the natural tendencies that lead us to indulge or simply put things off. Discipline is often the difference between what we want to be and what we actually are.


### Our Problems With Discipline

Most of us have a negative feeling about the word *discipline.* It sounds so rigid and boring. And it probably reminds us of childhood, when we were "disciplined" if we were bad. Unfortunately it's hard to

realize that as adults, discipline brings with it rewards—a trimmer body, more productivity, and even
better relationships. Perhaps the key is to stop calling it
discipline and start calling it control.

Control sounds a bit easier to me. It sounds rather
smooth and efficient. It reminds me of a sleek race car
taking a graceful turn or a ballet dancer poised on tip-
toe, her leg muscles taut and her body the picture of
grace.

Alan Lakein, in his book *How to Get Control of Your
Time and Your Life,* puts it well when he compares
control to the way you hold your hand. You can let
your hands go limp, leaving them useless, or you can
form them into tight fists, which gives you little ability
to function. But by flexing your fingers, you can use
your hands for countless activities, with control over
your movements.

I think that that is the way most of us want our lives
to be. We don't want to be so rigid and scheduled that
we can't have fun or be responsive. But neither are we
truly happy if we just let our lives go, with no control or
structure.

I am the kind of person who usually has several projects going at once. I seem to live on the edge of burnout
at times, yet I have consciously made the decision to
stay very busy. When someone questioned me about it
once, I gave them the real reason for my abundance of
activities. Fundamentally, I am an extremely lazy person. Given free time I will waste it. If I had my choice,
I would spend most days in bed until noon, reading
magazines, eating pastries, and listening to the stereo.

This really isn't a fantasy. Given a chance, my lazy tendencies take over and I am like the limp hand. I lose not only the ability, but also the inclination to do anything useful. My laziness perpetuates itself.

Of course, overinvolvement means that I'm really using external circumstances to control my laziness. One of my goals is to be more self-controlled so that I can more naturally follow the paths that lead to attaining my objectives (whether I *feel* like accomplishing the tasks or not).

### Steps Toward Discipline

I've always thought it was terribly unfair that "wishing doesn't make it so." I love to dream of all the things I would be if I could just wish them into existence. But the longer I live, the more I realize that wishing is not enough. If you really want something to happen, you have to work at it. And to work at something long enough and with enough endurance, you need discipline. Here are some steps to get you started:

### 1. *Recognize the need.*

I'll never forget a college friend of mine named Anne. She was one of the most beautiful women I've ever known and she had an incredible figure. Being around Anne tested my self-image, because men often stared openly as she walked by. One day Anne and I were having dinner in the school cafeteria, and I noticed that her tray was considerably less full than mine. She had a vegetable, a small piece of meat, and a glass of water. Although she'd never mentioned dieting, it suddenly occurred to me that Anne didn't have a great figure simply by chance. It sounds very naive, but at that point in my life, it never occurred to me that people worked at having a good figure.

Later, as Anne and I walked back to our dormitories, I asked her if she worked at staying in shape. "Of course," she said matter-of-factly. "I never eat desserts and I exercise every day." I remember my feelings of amazement at her attitude. For the first time in my life, I realized the full impact of control and the fallacy of "wishing can make it so."

All of us need discipline in our lives, yet it's easy to forget that it is an important and worthy objective. We sometimes drift along without taking responsibility for our actions, blaming outside circumstances for our inability to get things done. The first, and perhaps most obvious, step toward disicpline is simply confronting yourself with the fact that you need it. You are responsible for your life and you need to learn to discipline yourself if you are going to stay on course and stick to your plan. Simply wishing will *not* make it so. It takes work.

### 2. *Understand the benefits.*

The good news about discipline is that it is simply a means to an end. The end result is what's important and the steps you take to get there are just the pieces that add up to the total picture. When you think about the end results—the twenty-four-inch waist, or the completed diploma—it can seem like a massive accomplishment. But the fact is that most great accomplishments are simply made up of small steps taken one after another.

What we need to understand is that we cannot simply wake up one morning and find that all our discipline problems are solved. We have to work at the areas in which we lack control bit by bit. And that means that we have to educate ourselves. Our minds often play funny tricks on us. We convince ourselves that we have a lower metabolism, or an addiction to chocolate that keeps us from being thin. The fact is that we gain weight with every bite we take, and very rarely from some fundamental problem over which we have little control. If we can learn to control ourselves, one bit at a time, we have a chance at controlling our weight.

The same is true of the project at work that somehow keeps getting put off. Usually we have plenty of time to complete the assignment professionally if we begin to work on it right away and pace ourselves. But we get into trouble when the deadline sounds far away and we put off even thinking about the project. Then we pressure ourselves into doing a rush job that turns out to be less than we're capable of.

Sometimes lack of discipline is really lack of belief in one's self. We have all taken on an assignment thinking in the back of our minds, *I really can't do this. I'm scared.* With that kind of attitude we expend a great deal of energy on negative feelings. We begin to tell ourselves all the things we *aren't.* Because we see discipline as a positive trait, we remind ourselves of all the times we've failed to control our behavior. It can become an endless cycle of despair as we set ourselves up to fail and live *down* to the image we have created.

But in order to succeed at being disciplined we have to concentrate on the positive aspects. We have to remember all the things we can be when we incorporate control into our daily lives. We have to picture ourselves checking off the items on our "to do" lists; we have to remember the wonderful feeling of accomplishment.

Discipline can help move us toward our goals—if we remember the benefits.

### 3. *Control what you can.*

One of the rules I've learned about discipline is that I can control the big areas of my life better when I control some of the minor areas first. Let me explain. As you know from the examples I use in this book, I have a very difficult time controlling my weight. Of course, there are other areas of my life I have difficulty with, too, but dieting is often on my mind.

Recently I noticed that I was beginning to watch more and more television in the evening. I wasn't actually watching it, I was simply leaving it on while I played with my son, thumbed through a magazine, or caught up on sewing. But because it was on, my husband and I spent less time talking to each other, my son got only half of my attention, and I rarely remembered everything I'd read.

My husband and I decided to do something about what was becoming a bad habit. At first we considered going "cold turkey" for three weeks, but we each wanted to make exceptions. (He wanted to watch a few educational shows and I couldn't imagine missing "Dallas.") So instead we compromised on watching about four hours of television during the week (in addition to the nightly news). The rest of the time the TV would be shut off.

It hasn't been a really difficult test for us. We have to remind ourselves periodically to get up and switch off the set when the news is over, or we drift into "M*A*S*H" reruns, and then get hooked on prime-time sitcoms, but all in all, we're handling our new habit pretty well. We're gaining control over one area of our lives and we feel better about ourselves because of it.

The most exciting part of my disciplined television-viewing pattern is what control in that area has done for the rest of my life. I am beginning to see myself as a disciplined person. Every time I'm tempted to order a dessert, I remind myself of how good I feel about controlling my TV habit and how good I'll feel about controlling my weight. I begin to view myself in a new way—breaking out of those self-destructive patterns that keep me from living up to the image in which God created me.

### 4. *Make discipline a habit.*

When I first tried to learn to drive a manual-transmission car, I felt like the most uncoordinated person in the world. I panicked at the sight of an approaching hill, thinking I'd have to shift and use the clutch while rolling backward. I "killed" the car repeatedly in the first few weeks and often heard dreadful clanking and screeches as I tried to shift without using the clutch. The very worst experience was the day I had to park my car in a garage while attending a business meeting. When the meeting was over, more than 300 people left at the same time, creating a traffic jam in the garage. Waiting in line to leave was no problem. But when I neared the booth where I would pay, I was confronted with a steep incline. While dozens of people watched, I tried to inch up the hill, only to roll back again. Finally, in desperation, I put on the emergency brake and had the attendant drive my car out of the garage.

After driving a manual-transmission car for ten years now, it's hard for me to remember those days. Now every movement is automatic. I never think, *Okay, I have to ease out the clutch slowly now while pressing on the gas pedal.* It's an automatic response that I never analyze. That's how it can be with discipline in other areas of our lives.

One of the most exciting things is to realize how many areas of your life you already control. Think about the things you have learned to do automatically such as brushing your teeth, taking a shower, arriving at work on time, and preparing dinner. You probably don't think twice about doing these things every day. You don't lie in bed every morning and remind yourself that you really *should* get up and brush your teeth.

Make a list of all the things that you do control without a great deal of thought. My list includes arriving at work on time, watering my plants, cleaning the counter, and changing my baby's diaper regularly. These may all sound like insignificant tasks, but they all represent things I don't necessarily *want* to do, but I have learned to do regularly without thinking twice. I don't waste time trying to "psych" myself into doing them. Instead, they are now habits.

In order to be disciplined we have to learn more good habits and practice them regularly. We can make eating properly, daily exercise, and time management automatic responses instead of major accomplishments. They can become as much a part of our lives as brushing our teeth and making dinner. But in order to form a habit we have to practice it daily.

William James, one of the fathers of modern psychology, said that it takes twenty-one days of doing something repeatedly before it becomes a habit. Twenty-one days—three weeks—doesn't sound like a long time, but it is longer than the average length of time I stay on a diet, follow an exercise program, or maintain a daily "to do" list. At least that's how it used to be. Now I set twenty-one-day goals for myself, checking off the days in big red "X's" on a calendar. Instead of going on a crash diet for a week, I go on a more controlled diet for twenty-one days. In that amount of time I can easily lose five pounds—the amount of weight I often gain during vacations, busy times at work, or times of stress. And I don't immediately go back to my old ways, I've discovered, after three weeks of controlled eating. Instead I find that my stomach and mind have begun to accept less food as the norm. I have begun to form a good habit!

5.   *Build on your accomplishments.*

Every time you are able to control a difficult area in your life, give yourself a big pat on the back. Remind yourself of your accomplishment over and over again. Tell yourself that if you did it once you can do it again.

I went to graduate school at night while I was working full-time and found that going back to school was a very difficult process. I was out of my good study habits and was very involved in work and other activities. It took a real effort to make myself go to every class, I found homework agonizing, and I really suffered through many classes. But my ultimate goal—an M.B.A.—was very important to me.

In order to get my degree I had to take classes that were of little interest. And I had to drive to the university and back home late at night. There was no way around the fact that the only way I'd get my degree was simply to discipline myself and push ahead. I knew there'd be few rewards and many sacrifices before I received my diploma.

The only way I made it through the ordeal was by

gritting my teeth, praying regularly for stamina, and reminding myself of all the reasons why I wanted to finish graduate school. But I also found it helpful to keep track of how far I'd come, so I kept a chart of all the credits I needed to graduate. As I finished each course, I made a great ceremony of crossing off another group of credits. I congratulated myself on suffering through and thought about the investment I'd just made in my future.

As I worked on accounting problems late into the night, I reminded myself that I'd finished that tough economics class, so I could handle this one, too. I was determined to build on my accomplishments and make it through.

Yes, I finally finished graduate school and got my degree. It was never easy and rarely fun, but it was worth it. And one of the greatest benefits of having that diploma hanging on my wall is that every time I look at it I am reminded of how disciplined I had to be to make it through. I had to work at it, credit by credit, but I did it. And if I could accomplish such a difficult task as that, I should be able to do other things, too!

That's good news for me physically, mentally, and spiritually. When I glimpse my potential, I not only feel proud of myself, I also feel humbled by the magnificence of a God who could create me in His image and then give me the freedom to partake as fully as I want in the riches He has for me. I can choose to wander through life doing what I want when I want. But I can also "tap in" to the master plan God has for me. When I do, I discover that discipline really means more than control; it means freedom. And the more I practice the art of discipline, the more I am free to be the person God has in mind.

\* \* \* \*

As you take steps toward becoming a more disciplined person ask yourself:

1. Why do I want to discipline my life? Do I *really* want to gain control?
2. What will my life be like when I'm more disciplined? What are all the tasks I will accomplish?
3. What areas of my life do I control already? In what ways am I a disciplined person already?
4. What are some of the "easy" things I can learn to control? What exactly will I do about them over the next three weeks?
5. What are the bigger areas of my life I can learn to discipline? How will I feel when I form good habits in those areas?

# 9. *Recognizing Opportunities*

Whearing I first met Barbara I was impressed by the ever-present smile on her face and her generally enthusiastic response to life. As I got to know her, I was even more impressed by the many things she had already accomplished. She had traveled extensively all over the world, met famous people, and worked at some prestigious and exciting jobs. And I had the distinct impression that all she'd done so far was only the beginning of what she would do in the future.

After knowing Barbara I was interested to hear how other people described her. Some called her dynamic, others said she was talented and creative. But one person used the word *lucky* to describe her. Perhaps the obvious reason for the label was the fact that Barbara's parents are well-known people. Because of their status, she has had many opportunities to travel, meet interesting people, and get her "foot in the door" of places where she wanted to work. Barbara even considers herself lucky for the many options that have come her way. But if luck were all Barbara had going for her, she would be a far less interesting person than she is.

Barbara is like many successful people whom others try to analyze. "She's just been lucky" is an easy way to justify the fact that she has done more than most women ever dream of accomplishing. Yet it obviously takes more than luck to accomplish something. It takes planning, discipline, the ability to manage time—*and* the ability to recognize and seize opportunities. It's that ability that is often described as luck. But every one of us can be "lucky" if we learn to spot the possibilities that come our way and turn them into concrete achievements.

I'm not just talking about career opportunities that open doors to the next promotion. I'm talking about any circumstances that arise in daily life that help us take steps toward our goals.

For example, the subway system in the Washington, D.C., area is expanding to the suburbs and a new station recently opened near my house. I read about the event with little interest since I drive to work every day and park in the lot beside my building. It's a convenient and fast commute for me, so there was little reason to consider paying the high subway fare and sitting on a train that stopped a dozen times before reaching a station a few blocks from my office.

But then I began to realize that I needed to do something about my backlog of reading materials. It was important for me to stay informed, but I couldn't find time in my daily schedule to fit in the reading. That's when I remembered the new subway stop. Now I take the train at least one day a week whenever my reading material piles up. The extra hour and a half of reading time clears up quite a pile of magazines and correspondence. And in the end, taking the train really only costs me an extra half-hour of time and a few dollars—well worth it to help me achieve my goal.

This may all sound very basic to you, but recently I was discussing a story I'd read in a magazine, and someone asked me how much time I spent each week reading current publications. When I said that I tried to spend at least one or two hours, the person said, "You're really *lucky* to have so much time to devote to reading." I had to laugh to myself at that comment. Luck had little to do with it. Obviously I am lucky that the subway station opened near my house, but that was just a fact until I realized that it was an opportunity.

In order to become a lucky person—one who recognizes and seizes opportunities—you have to have the proper perspective. First of all you have to know what's important to you, what your goals and priorities are and what you're trying to achieve. Then you have to be open to the many circumstances that present themselves to you each day. And finally you have to be prepared to act on them when the timing and conditions are right.

### Opening Up to Opportunity

The process that started you dreaming is very similar to the process that can start you down the road to recognizing opportunities. In both cases you need to learn to open yourself up to all your life can be. You need to learn to think creatively and imagine the future as you would like it to be.

Let me tell you about two friends of mine, Sara and Janice. Sara is a wonderful, kind person whom all of her friends appreciate. But Sara also seems to be very unlucky. Nothing ever seems to go her way.

Janice, on the other hand, is almost always excited about something that is happening to her. She always seems to be discovering a wonderful new recipe or finding a great new baby-sitter or getting a terrific job offer.

It might seem on the surface that Janice is simply lucky, while Sara has bad luck. But a closer look at both of them points out the real difference. When a new circumstance happens to Sara, she tends to view it as a problem or a burden. When her boss gives her a new assignment, she feels overworked. When her apartment building became a condominium, she felt victimized.

In turn, we all expect bad things to happen to Sara. Whenever she calls, I mentally prepare myself for bad news. And she rarely lets me down.

Although Janice has her share of problems, she views every new situation as an opportunity rather than a setback. Every new task at the office becomes a chance to develop a new skill or learn a new area. When her husband lost his job recently, she used her newly reduced food budget to experiment with vegetarian dishes and tofu.

Obviously, the biggest difference between my two friends is their attitudes. One is open to opportunities; the other isn't. Janice is determined to find a way to learn, benefit, and grow, while Sara expects only the worst to come her way.

### Being Prepared

Earlier we discussed the problem of "overplanning" your life to the point that you aren't open to circumstances. But having walked through the exercises in which you learned more about yourself and your goals, you are probably beginning to understand that too much planning is rarely a problem.

Life is so full of options that on any given day you have to be able to use some guidelines for making choices or you can get caught racing in a dozen different directions. In order to make your dreams come true you have to be selective about what you say yes to. You have to know what moves you in the right direction and what diverts you.

The best preparation for dealing with daily decisions is having a firm grip on your goals. If being a good wife is one of my top goals and I read about a marriage seminar being offered at my church, I can view it as an opportunity. If I am invited to address a women's conference on a weekend when I had planned to be home with my husband, I have to make a hard decision about its value. But at least I have prepared myself for the decision by walking through my priorities and values and knowing what my goals are. By establishing my goals I have increased my sensitivity to those things that help my life move forward.

### Where Opportunities Come From

Recently I opened my mailbox and found an envelope with large red letters proclaiming, "Enclosed—a wonderful opportunity for you and your family." If only it were that easy to spot an opportunity! Not many come marked with large red letters or with an announcement. Instead we have to spot them, name them, and then pursue them before they really become opportunities.

Opportunities can originate through people, circumstances, or even within ourselves. They may come in the mailbox or through the seed of an idea that starts in our mind and blooms into a creative concept. In fact some of the best opportunities arise through the shuffling of thoughts that occurs as we dream. As you add new material to your dream file and review ideas from the past, doesn't your mind start to work creatively? Do you begin to think "What if . . ." thoughts? I do. In fact I often find that when I return from vacation, very exciting things start happening to me. Part of the reason is that when I go on vacation I tend to relax and let my mind work creatively. I'm often reminded of an idea to pursue, a person to contact, or a new approach to take. I read books that stimulate my thinking. I take long walks and let my mind sift through options. And when I return home I begin to follow up on the ideas that occurred to me on vacation.

It's exciting to see how many opportunities come my way after I have relaxed and brainstormed for a few days. My creative thinking results in some very tangible options that often help me take steps toward my goals.

Another way that opportunities come our way is through other people. Every once in a while, I meet someone whose mind and ideas stimulate me in a new way. Sometimes this person is interested in an area I've never known about and his or her enthusiasm rubs off on me. I often discover a new interest or hobby or begin to read books in a new subject area.

A friend of mine named Vickie first introduced me to an appreciation of antique magazine covers. I admired the beautiful covers she had framed in her home, and she began to tell me about their significance and rarity. As she talked, her excitement was contagious, and I came to appreciate the prints in a new way.

A few months later I was wandering through a shopping mall when I came upon an antique show. Normally I would have passed it by, but I saw an exhibit of old prints, advertisements, and magazines. I stopped because of the excitement I'd "caught" from Vickie and was delighted to find some rare and beautiful magazine covers that now hang on my walls. Without the understanding I gained from Vickie, I would have passed that opportunity by. But she opened a whole new area to me.

There has been a great deal of talk lately about "networking," which usually means making contact with people who can help further your career. Networking is really another word for opportunity gathering—a way of getting to know people who open doors, stimulate thinking, or share ideas.

Whether you call it networking or not, you still meet people each and every day who can help you move toward the goals you've established for yourself. By learning from them and opening yourself up to what they have to say, you can find new opportunities for growth. You can find new energy and creative approaches that will help you make your dreams come true.

### How to Respond

Let's imagine that you wake up tomorrow morning with your eyes wide open to opportunities that might come your way. You listen, observe, and analyze everything with an eye toward how it can help you learn and grow. How do you respond when what you think is an opportunity comes your way?

First, you must remember your current priorities. You have to replay your goals daily to establish and reestablish what is important in your life at this time.

You have to commit yourself to those goals and judge opportunities on the basis of how they conform to those goals, and learn to say no to potential diversions. As I said before, it is often difficult to differentiate between an opportunity and a diversion initially. But as you become more skilled in analyzing your options, you will more readily see whether they will help or hinder your progress.

For example, I was recently offered the opportunity to coauthor a book with a man whom I greatly admire. I was convinced that by helping him put his ideas into a book, I would learn a great deal and that we would make an important contribution to the lives of men and women around the world.

I took a long, hard look at my goals and knew that there was very little to support my involvement in the project. Although the benefits might be great in the long run, it would take time and energy away from specific commitments—short-term goals—I had already made to my family. It was a very difficult decision, but I said no.

A month later an opportunity arose that once again was time-consuming and exciting. But this was a chance to work on something with my husband in a way that would contribute directly to our goals for our marriage. I gladly said yes to this new project and reminded myself that I couldn't have become involved if I had already committed myself to the first project.

Analyzing your priorities is just the first step in responding to an opportunity. You also have to believe in yourself and your ability to accomplish something in a new area. Sometimes, even though an option seems consistent with your goals, it is overwhelming and intimidating.

When my friend Joan was offered a new job that would take her toward her goal of becoming a manager in her company, she tried to find a dozen reasons to turn it down.

"I haven't really learned all I can in my present job," she reasoned. "Besides, I just don't think I'm qualified. I'd do a terrible job in that position." Those of us who knew Joan realized that her boss had seen potential and believed in her ability to handle the new job. Of course she hadn't learned *everything* about her current position and naturally she wouldn't walk in to the new job and understand it thoroughly from the start. But Joan was hardworking and bright and would learn her new duties quickly.

Joan was also scared and had a hard time believing in herself. She lacked the self-confidence she needed to take advantage of opportunities that came her way. As a result, she often talked herself right out of wonderful chances to grow and take steps toward her goal.

Fear of failure and lack of self-confidence are two of the greatest obstacles to overcome when you are faced with a new option. If a new option seems to be in keeping with your goals, follow a principle my husband taught me: Say yes until you have to say no. Don't worry about the ultimate effect of your decision. Take a step at a time, reminding yourself of how far you've come already.

Once you've started recognizing opportunities and

moving foward, you'll be surprised at how many more seem to spring up. If you have a desire to grow and a willingness to respond to life's many options, you'll become attuned to opportunities as they come your way and you'll be able to respond enthusiastically to them. You'll find that the evaluation process becomes nearly automatic. And you'll find that each step you take helps you gain confidence in your ability to accomplish great things in the future.

Remember my two friends, Sara and Janice? Janice has learned to say yes to life and its many opportunities. She understands her priorities, has confidence in her abilities, and is willing to grow and move forward.

Janice is learning to make her dreams come true— and so can you!

*    *    *    *

Ask yourself these questions relating to opportunities that come your way.

1. Whom do I know whom I consider "lucky"? Can I find reasons for their good luck?
2. Have I formulated my goals and reaffirmed what I value?
3. Do I have time to think creatively?
4. Whom do I know who stimulates my thinking and helps open new areas for me?
5. Do I believe in myself? Am I ready to say yes to opportunity and take it a step at a time?

# 10. Reaching Out to Others

In order to assess your life, set your goals, and move toward them, you need the help of others. You need to lean on your family, rely on your friends, and ask the help of people you may hardly know.

But there's another way you need others if you're really going to make your dreams come true. You need other people to reach out to and share yourself with. To be a really fulfilled person you need to give of yourself.

Once you've taken stock of your life you should have a new sense of confidence in your abilities and your priorities. This should free you to take a look around and help others reach their goals, too. You don't need to wait until you've progressed very far in your own life planning to reach out. As soon as you begin to give of

147

yourself, you'll find an amazing thing happens—you'll want to give even more because it makes you feel so good.

There's absolutely nothing that makes you feel as good about yourself as wholeheartedly reaching out to others. Even when you don't get praise or credit, an act of kindness—of reaching and stretching for the good of someone else—helps you grow as a person.

Reaching out and helping others has a way of developing self-confidence. As you are able to make someone else feel loved and wanted, you begin to believe in yourself. You know that you can make a difference in someone's life and this helps you believe in your ability to handle your own problems, too!

I once heard a minister tell the story of a lonely woman who came to him for counseling. She was suffering from severe depression and was so mentally distressed that she had become physically ill. Although she had visited several doctors, no one seemed to be able to help. By the time she visited the minister, she was convinced that she was dying.

Knowing that she had been tested by doctors, the minister reasoned that the woman's problems could stem from her mental and spiritual situation. After spending many hours talking to her, he discovered that materially she lacked nothing; yet her life seemed totally aimless. She spent most of her days in bed, watching television or reading magazines.

The minister's prescription for the woman was amazingly simple: She was to spend an hour each day at the local orphanage helping the children in any way she could.

When the minister met the woman again less than a year later, he was amazed at the difference. She looked healthy and energetic. There was a bounce to her step and her eyes shone. She was brimming with enthusiasm as she told him about a little boy who was learning to read because of her patience with him and a girl who was learning to smile again. When the minister inquired about the woman's own problems, she looked confused for a moment and then laughed.

"I've never felt better in my life," she said. I guess I was just spending too much time thinking about me and not enough time thinking about anyone else."

We are all guilty of getting too self-absorbed from time to time. Concentrating on ourselves can undermine our confidence, drive us to depression, and even lead to physical illness. Even concentrating on our personal goals to the exclusion of others' needs keeps us from being truly whole people.

Never get so caught up in making your dreams come true that you forget about others who need you. It's easy to focus on a goal and put on blinders to other people. But along with your quest for fulfillment you have an obligation to help others find happiness, too. Whether you help physically, mentally, or spiritually, you give of yourself in a way that returns to you many times over.

The Bible says, "Whoever wants to be great among you must be your servant" (*see* Luke 22:26). True fulfillment really does come from helping others on a day-to-day basis. It helps you keep your life in perspective while you focus on becoming all you can be.

Just in case you're having a hard time imagining ways you can reach out, here are ten suggestions.

1. *Reach out from your strength.* Having gone through an assessment of your skills, you should have a fairly good idea of where you excel and what talents you already have. Try to think of all the ways you can help others through the skills and talents God has given you.

If you're a good cook, volunteer to help with the bake sale at your children's school or offer to cook an extra dish for the church dinner. If you excel in sports, perhaps you can teach a group of handicapped youngsters to swim or you could lead your neighbors in an aerobics class.

Learn to build on your strengths and share them with others. Doing so will give you confidence in yourself and will remind you of your unique gifts.

2. *Reach out from your weakness.* When I interviewed Rebecca Manley Pippert recently, the best-selling author had just moved from Washington, D.C., to Israel. Her husband, Wes, is a correspondent for United Press International and when a wonderful position opened up for him they decided to move without a moment's hesitation.

When Becky arrived in Israel, she discovered that the adjustment was far more difficult than she had anticipated. First, no one knew of her there. They weren't clamoring to hear her speak or asking her to autograph her book. Furthermore, she related to people more as the wife of Wes than on her own as she had in the past. It all added up to a very lonely situation for Becky.

But after much prayer, Becky felt that God was teaching her a lesson: She was to learn to reach out from her weakness rather than her strength. Knowing that her greatest weakness at the time was loneliness, she decided that she would try to help others who needed friends. So she organized a luncheon for all the other wives of foreign correspondents.

The response to Becky's luncheon was overwhelming. Nearly every woman who attended confessed that she, too, was lonely and that Becky's gesture had really helped. Becky became friends with many of the women and by helping them alleviated her problem, too.

Is there an area of your life that you would like to develop, or a problem you'd like to overcome? Perhaps you can find a way to reach out to others who share your problem and in doing so help yourself, too. One woman who was suffering from abuse by her husband started a support group for women who had similar problems. Another woman had a problem sticking to her diet, so she found a friend who shared her problem and encouraged her friend (and herself) to a slim new figure.

Whatever your weakness, learn to spot it, understand it, and help others with the same problem. You'll be surprised at how reaching out helps!

3. *Reach out to those close to you.* Sometimes the most difficult people to reach out to are those who are closest to you. As the old saying goes, "Charity begins at home," but sometimes home is the last place you feel like sharing yourself with others.

Serving your husband, children, or roommate can

seem like the most thankless task on earth. It often seems as though you give and give and no one even notices. And worst of all, those at home often come to *expect* you to give.

One of the problems I often have is that I want to give in the way *I* want to instead of giving to a family member as he or she is needy. Recently, I decided to observe my family for a week and try to see them through new eyes. I wanted to see what *they* wanted, not what *I* wanted to give. I discovered some significant differences when I looked at my husband that way. I'd always imagined that "gourmet" dinners were important to him. But what I came to realize was that he preferred time alone with me to elaborate meals. While I was feeling like a martyr for slaving away in the kitchen, he was frustrated because we had so little time alone. Now we spend a quiet half-hour talking before I prepare one of the "jiffy" meals I've incorporated into my recipe file.

If you want to give of yourself to others, start by looking at the needs of those closest to you. Try to look at them with new eyes. Try to understand their needs as *they* feel them. And then learn to meet those needs in a way that helps them grow. I think you'll be surprised by how much *you* grow in the process!

4.   *Reach out to those far away.*   It's easy to get very comfortable when you live in a land of plenty as most of us do. I can't remember ever going hungry because I lacked money for food (except in college when I squandered my food allowance on a new pair of shoes). And I've certainly never lacked for a warm winter coat

or boots or gloves. But because of my comfort I often forget that many people lack the basics of life.

Children in my city and in Third World countries go to bed hungry. Adults starve or freeze to death every winter. I don't like to think of those harsh realities, but they do exist and I have a responsibility to remember those men, women, and children. That's why I need to reach out to those who are far away from me—whether overseas or simply miles away in a ghetto. Reaching out to them also reminds me of how fortunate I am; it puts my life and my goals in perspective.

When I supported a child overseas for a few years, I rarely read his letters without tears coming to my eyes. I cried because I felt so fortunate to have all that I had. But I also felt glad that the few dollars I sent each month meant so much to him. For less than the cost of a new scarf I provided him with two meals each day for a month. What a unique and fulfilling opportunity. How small my problems seemed compared to his!

5. *Reach out to those like you.* It's very tempting to envy those who are most like us. I admire my neighbor's new car (and secretly wish I had one). I congratulate my co-worker on her promotion (and wonder why I didn't get one). People who are like us entice us into the trap of comparisons. And when we begin to compare, we can't help but lose.

The opposite of envy, jealousy, and comparison is service. If you learn to reach out and serve those most like you, you will find yourself growing in great leaps and bounds. You will find that you are genuinely happy for your neighbor, and you'll cheer your co-worker on as she proceeds up the corporate ladder.

It won't be easy. Helping those who are like you is probably the most difficult thing to do. We often find the traits that we dislike in ourselves the most annoying in others. And we readily find fault in those who are most like us.

But helping someone who is like you will stretch you in a new way and will probably do more than anything else to help you accept yourself.

6. *Reach out to those different from you.* Have you ever known someone whom you just couldn't figure out? Someone who seemed motivated by forces you just didn't understand? I had a neighbor like that once. I tried for months to find some common ground, but I finally decided that she and I had absolutely nothing in common.

Faced with this situation I did the only thing I could: I continued to listen to Emily for a clue to her needs. After weeks of seemingly aimless conversations I began to discover that Emily barely made ends meet toward the end of each month. She was far too proud to reveal the problem, but the signs began to add up. I was convinced that asking Emily about it would only make her self-conscious, so I began to develop a strategy. Toward the end of each month I'd plan a meal of a large roast or I'd double a casserole or spaghetti recipe. Then I'd casually call Emily about the problem I had of an overfull freezer or extra meat that was sure to spoil. Sometimes I'd give Emily a batch of cents-off coupons I'd clipped or received in the mail. I think Emily finally realized that I knew her problem. But for months she said nothing and when I finally moved, she gave me a very warm hug and thanked me "for everything" again and again. Emily and I were as different as night and day. But we shared a bond based on her need, and it made us both feel good about ourselves and each other.

Dr. Norman Vincent Peale made famous the phrase, "Find a need and fill it." Sometimes it takes time to spot a need in someone so different from yourself. But finding that need and filling it can create a bond of friendship and a means of growth.

7. *Reach out to the needy.* I have an office that overlooks a busy street in Washington. I'm a habitual people watcher and sometimes I invent games about the people walking by. Some days I try to guess their job; other days I imagine what their husband or wife is like. But some days I try to imagine what their greatest need is. In an affluent city like Washington the need is rarely material. Sometimes it's the confusion of not knowing what bus stops at the corner. Other times it's a look of concern—possibly about a pending business deal. The point is that everyone is needy in one way or another. Perhaps they aren't wearing tattered shoes, but they may be in inner turmoil over a problem.

Look for the need in each person you come in contact with. Learn to be sensitive to the signs of distress, the symptoms of need. Then, as best you can, reach out to that person and help meet those needs.

8. *Reach out to those without apparent needs.* It might sound strange to talk about men and women who have no needs, but we've all known people who were very good at covering up any weakness or hurt.

Sometimes they're the happy type who never seem to be bothered by anything. Other times they're the stoics who steadfastly set their jaw and keep a stiff upper lip.

Once I heard a minister's wife describe her situation. She explained that she was always supposed to smile and act warmly toward the people in the church—even those who she knew were critical of her husband. She was supposed to offer a shoulder to cry on to anyone who needed it. And she was never, ever supposed to show any need or weakness. Keeping up this facade took its toll mentally and physically on her. She was a very needy person, but was totally unable to show her needs. Because of that, no one ever reached out to her.

"If only one person in the congregation had seen through my mask and tried to help me, it would have made all the difference in the world," she told me tearfully.

I knew a man once who never showed any emotion. He worked in a company where I was a summer secretary during high school, and we all joked about him behind his back. We even used to try to tease him into some display of emotion—without success. Then one day John started acting very strangely. He hid under his desk and begged us not to tell the police that he was there. Within one day he literally fell apart before our eyes, showing the entire range of emotions he'd never before exhibited.

In the aftermath of John's breakdown we all felt guilty about our cruel treatment of him. Obviously, John's needs were there and were, perhaps, beyond our ability to help. But we could have offered him comfort instead of criticism. We could have reached out to him even if he wasn't asking for help in any way we understood.

Is there someone in your life who seems to have no needs at all? Does he or she seem totally well-adjusted or completely stoic? Don't accept his or her attitude as the final word. Offer a kind word or an understanding comment whenever you can.

9. *Reach out from your pain.* Whenever you experience a painful situation it's natural to pull inward. The pain of loss, humiliation, or betrayal is nearly impossible to share with someone else. But when you do experience pain, the very best thing you can do is turn around and open yourself up even more by helping others who have experienced similar pain.

The tragic loss of a child to an accident or disease has led many parents to form organizations to find cures or ways to prevent the loss of other lives. Through the death of their child they've learned to help others not only deal with a similar situation, but also prevent deaths in the future.

On a smaller scale, most of us experience pain through daily incidents such as the betrayal of a friend or the embarrassment of a social blunder. We can react to the pain of such incidents by closing ourselves off and steeling ourselves to criticism. Or we can learn and grow from the situation and help someone else who is suffering in a similar way.

I remember my first full-time professional position as if it were yesterday. I made every mistake in the book during my first month on the job and went home every night with tears in my eyes, feeling foolish and hurt by my blunders. Eventually I improved and even came to feel fairly competent. But I never forgot those first-job feelings of pain.

Recently a woman came to work for me who reminded me of myself during those early days. I could see her frustration and understand her pain. So one day we talked. I told her about the things that had happened to me during that first job, the pain I had felt and my sense of humiliation. I assured her that it would get better and I tried to comfort her through her difficult growth phase. It still hurt as I talked about my blunders. But I felt a sense of satisfaction as I realized how much I had grown since those days—and how I was able to help someone else learn from my pain.

10. *Reach out from your pleasure.* Perhaps it's a natural reaction for you to share your joy and good fortune with others. But that's not always the automatic way to respond. Many of us can get greedy about the good that comes our way. We want to enjoy it ourselves and not share it with others.

The next time something good happens to you, use the happiness you receive from it to reach out to someone else. When you receive a compliment, turn around and give one to someone else. When you feel good about achieving a goal, turn around and help someone else reach her goal. Reaching out from your pleasure will never dilute your enjoyment. It will enhance it, expand it, and give you more opportunities to enjoy it.

As you begin to dream and make those dreams come true, remember to share your good fortune and increased confidence. Help others learn what you have. Reach out to those who need encouragement and compassion. For to be a truly fulfilled person your dreams need to include others.

*       *       *       *       *

It *is* a wonderful time to be a woman! Although the future may not be ours to see, we know that our options are greater than ever before. And by using some of the tools in this book we can move forward with confidence that we are doing everything we can to make our dreams come true.

God has given each one of us unique talents and abilities and placed us in our particular circumstances for a reason. He brings new opportunities into our lives every day and continually offers us chances to grow and stretch.

In order to move forward we have to take responsibility for our lives and our talents. We have to acknowledge our strengths, work on our weaknesses, and challenge ourselves. We have to learn to dream big dreams. And we have to learn that, with God's help, we *can* make our dreams come true.